EAST

Nicola Slee was born in 1958 and spent her childhood in North Devon. The changing moods of the seasons, reflected in land and sea, have always been important to her. She studied theology and educational psychology at Cambridge and currently lectures in religious studies at the Roehampton Institute of Higher Education. She has wide-ranging interests in theology and education, and a number of previous publications.

Easter Garden

A Sequence of Readings on the
Resurrection Hope

Compiled and Introduced by
NICOLA SLEE

Collins
FOUNT PAPERBACKS

First published in Great Britain by Fount Paperbacks,
London in 1990

Copyright © Nicola Slee 1990

Printed and bound in Great Britain by
William Collins Sons & Co. Ltd, Glasgow

For Jo, Kate and Leslie

The new creation, like the old, begins in a garden.

Douglas Webster

He brought me into a deep remembering garden
And I was like one that wakes from a dream of pain
To hear the cry of a thrush in the woods at evening
And the sound of a brook and the whisper of Eden
  again.

Alfred Noyes

Contents

Preface

Growth in the natural world is a slow and mysterious process, much of it secret and hidden from observation. The growth of plant life begins underground, in the darkness and hiddenness of the soil, where the buried seed lies inert, apparently dead, waiting for moisture and warmth to stir it into life. What finally emerges from the soil weeks or months later bears little or no resemblance to the small, shrivelled, insignificant thing from which it began its life, yet there can be no life without it.

The growth of this collection of readings has also been a slow and largely secret process, starting from the small seed of an idea and taking some seven years to grow from its seed-like inception to its final flowering in print. As seeds begin to sprout in darkness, so the beginnings of the anthology took root during a bleak and wintry season in my own life. Death and divorce in the family and the departure of a close friend to a distant part of the country, just when I felt I needed the friendship most, precipitated a lengthy period of darkness and depression. It seemed as if all that had been safe, trusted and secure in my life had suddenly, come crashing down around me. I had not realized how much my sense of value and identity had depended on those foundations of family, home and friendship until, suddenly, they were not there. Without them, I felt lost, confused and uncertain of my life. I wrestled and raged against God. I did not understand why God had allowed it all to happen. I wanted God to pick up the pieces, stick them all back together again, wave his magic wand and make everything better again, as if none of it had ever happened, and he would not, he would not do it.

After months of angry denial and confusion, I began to learn to accept the darkness, welcome the wounds, and begin the slow, painful journey towards healing and wholeness, towards integration of the darkness into my life. I never doubted that God was with me in the struggle, but I had to learn that God would not rescue me from the pain and the confusion, as I so desperately wanted him to do; rather, the resurrection I was seeking for my own life could only come about by entering into the darkness and submitting to its terror, believing, against all hope, that new life could be born from the hidden depths.

Finally there came a time when I began to sense the stirrings of new life and confidence within my battered self. This time in my life corresponded to the seasons' waking from the cold darkness of winter and turning towards the newness of spring. It was early March in Cambridge. All along the backs of the colleges, where the Cam flows under willows, the grass was dotted and specked with bursts of yellow aconites and flashes of white snowdrops, and the deep velvet of golden and purple crocuses was beginning to show. The air was crisp and keen as it can be only in the chilly Eastern counties, piercing the dullness of the senses and carrying the freshness of spring scents with it. Spring in Cambridge is always beautiful, and it was my sixth year in the city; yet that spring was like my first, like the world's first springtime ever, so sharply and keenly did I experience the season's beauty. I read it as a sign of coming resurrection, a foretaste of what God could and would do in my own life.

At about this time, I came across two books which spoke to me deeply. The first was *The Secret Garden*, by Frances Hodgson Burnett, given to me by a friend. I had not read the book as a child, and now I read the tale of Mary Lennox's discovery of beauty and healing in the locked and abandoned garden with a sense of mounting excitement. I identified with the lonely, confused, orphaned child, and read her story of gradual transformation as a sign of the transformation that could take place in my own life. The second book was Rowan Williams' *Resurrection*, and I was particularly struck by the chapter exploring the Johannine narrative of Mary Magdalene's encounter with the risen Christ in the garden. Rowan Williams makes much of Mary's turning and returning to the grave, her going back to the place of the wounded and buried past, and shows how Mary's refusal to abandon the apparently hopeless memory leads, at last, to an answering recognition of her own woundedness and need, to a moment of healing and restoration of self. I identified with the wounded, broken woman returning to the grave, and read her story of welcome and healing as a sign of the welcome and healing God was offering me.

Reading the two books, the two Mary stories, and hearing an echo of these stories of resurrection everywhere in the springtime around me, marked a transition, a turning point, in my journey out of depression and towards healing. I read of the child and the woman welcomed, healed, named, transformed, and felt myself welcomed, healed, named and transformed with them. I walked the streets of Cambridge, dazzled by the sharp, crisp air, the sun

on my face and hands, the first green tips of buds
showing, the almost painful purity and intensity
of colour in the spring flowers, the sweet, heady
fragrance of earth and things growing, and sensed
all the world dripping with its "juice and joy". In
all that I was reading, as well as in all that I was
seeing, hearing, touching, smelling, tasting in the
new season, there was an unmistakable message of
new life emerging out of barrenness and death, hope
springing up where despair and chaos had reigned. I
read, I looked, I believed and joyfully accepted the
resurrection tidings.

A few weeks later, and having finished reading
the books, I joined others on the end of term college
retreat at the diocesan retreat house at Pleshey. I
don't remember much about what was said in the
addresses, but I do remember the healing silence
and welcoming warmth of the house and those who
lived there. I went out walking one afternoon into
the flat, open, Essex landscape. It was a still, dry,
grey afternoon. Against the vast dome of whitish
sky, every line and twist of tree, hedgerow and
bush was etched in startling clarity, like a painter's
brushstrokes showing clear on the canvas. I walked
slowly and looked carefully at the growing grasses,
trees and bushes. In striking contrast to the lush,
riotous colour and scents of the Cambridge backs,
this was not a landscape to dazzle or overwhelm,
but one to quieten and deepen, demanding slow and
deliberate attention. Here, the colours were muted,
the only sounds of birdsong were thin and distant,
tossed into the great bowl of sky, where they seemed
to dissolve into the air, and the shapes of trees,
hedges and fields were dwarfed by this one, over-
mastering presence of sky. I stopped by a hedge and

looked at the trees growing there, thin and white and wiry, with no green showing. I picked a slim, white branch which looked more like bone than living tree, and marvelled that out of this apparently dead, brittle, pale hardness shoots of lush green would soon emerge. There was no sign of sap or green anywhere in the branch I held in my hand, and yet I knew it would sprout green soon. Standing there, under the huge sky with this dry, brittle bit of tree in my hand, suddenly I knew with an overwhelming sense of certainty that, despite all signs to the contrary, my own life would sprout green again soon. With this knowledge of certitude came a great rush of words, seemingly out of nowhere, spoken out of the silence of the sky. I rushed back to the house and the words of a poem came tumbling on to the page, whole:

And can these dry bones live?
these bare boughs sprout green?
In my hand the twigs snap –
no sign of living sap –
and each stalk
is sharp, dry as chalk,
scratches blood
with the hard knot of wood.

And can these dry boughs live?
Yes, since one tree of death
bore love's last breath
  (no harder wood
  no bleaker bough
  no sharper thorn
  we'll ever know)
and flamed with the fruit of Christ's risen body

on the first Good Sunday,
all trees on earth partake this miracle,
proclaim this glory.

Look long, then, here, at this
budding of dead wood:
and in our lives,
however dry or gnarled the grain,
he'll cause the flower of love
to sprout again.

Writing the poem itself was an extraordinary experience of affirmation and wholeness, a great rush of life and creativity which I received as gift and grace, a powerful assurance of the healing and restoration that God would work in me. I knew that there would still be plenty of struggle and darkness to come, that the growing had hardly begun, yet I also knew with a striking certainty and clarity of vision that I could trust God's goodness to work the same miracle of regeneration in me that I saw in the natural world around me.

Following this experience, I felt I wanted to make some kind of tangible response to all this gift and grace I had been given: the gift of springtime in Cambridge, the gift of the two Marys' stories, the gift of the poem and the healing in my own life it represented. I wanted to share something of this gift with others in a tangible, concrete form. I also wanted to do some further work on the two Mary stories and on all this imagery of growth, healing, transformation and resurrection which seemed to be shouting out all around me and stirring powerfully within me. I had the idea of putting together a sequence of readings, centred around the two

Mary stories, for performance during Eastertide in the college chapel, as a way of sharing something of the Easter process of transformation with others. So the anthology was born. I hunted out poems, passages of scripture, prose extracts and prayers which explored the process of growth in the natural world or reflected on the Mary stories in some other way. Together with a number of friends, a sequence of readings, with music and silence, was created and performed in Selwyn College chapel during Eastertide 1983.

I thought that this performance would bring to an end my work on the material, but I found that, if anything, it only deepened and rekindled my interest and involvement. I did not want to part company with either of the Marys; I wanted to explore their stories further, sensing that my own story was intimately connected with theirs. And so the anthology has grown with me. I have worked at it, on and off, since 1983; collecting fresh extracts here and there, discarding some passages for others, making notes and working on the connections between the two Mary stories and the larger story of the passion, death and resurrection of Christ.

From the initial planting of the seed of an idea in the spring of 1983 to its fruition in 1990, many people have helped to tend, nurture and, where necessary, prune, the growing plant! I am grateful to Sue Chapman, Gavin D'Costa, Chris Harrison, Kate Lees, Janet Morley, Lesley Riddle, Robert Titley and Lesley Walmsley for their careful reading of the manuscript at various stages of its growth, their searching out of extracts or copyright details, and especially for their helpful comments. Thanks are also due to Jo Granger, who patiently typed and retyped sections of the manuscript, and to Anne King, who cleared copyright permissions and prepared the typescript for publication. There are, however, three people who have made a special contribution to this book by their support, encouragement and faith in me, without which I could not have written what follows. I am deeply grateful to them. Jo Jones made this anthology possible by the gift of *The Secret Garden* when I needed a sign of hope, and has gifted me with her constant friendship, even when I have least deserved it. Kate Grillet helped me work on the imagery of growth in the secret garden and come to a place in my own life where I could see the "sharp little pale green points" emerging out of the darkness of the soil. With great patience and understanding, Leslie Francis bore the brunt of much of my anger and despair during the bleakest, coldest time of the wintry season, and never failed to believe in me. To Jo, Kate and Leslie, whose love tended the garden, I offer what follows.

Nicola Slee,
Whitelands College,
Eastertide 1989

Introduction

The Easter experience – life out of death

"Christ is risen! He is risen indeed, alleluia!" This resounding proclamation of the resurrection of the crucified one, chanted by Christians the world over on Easter Day, is the heart and centre of Christian faith, at once its seed and its flower, the root and branch of Christian believing. Year by year the Christian Church celebrates the Easter story as the climax and goal of its liturgical calendar, and as the essential key to human knowledge of and encounter with God. Week by week and day by day, in the central act of Christian worship, the same story of passion, self-offering, vindication and victory is enacted and proclaimed as bread is taken, offered, broken and shared, and Christ's death and resurrection celebrated in the company of God's people. Year by year, week by week and day by day, Christians are called to reflect upon the Easter events, to celebrate their victory and to appropriate their meaning and message for their own lives. In prayer, worship, work and every aspect of life, Christians are called to consent to the Eastering Spirit moulding, shaping and renewing their lives. However variously Christians interpret and understand the original Easter events, they are agreed that it is here, in these strange and troubling happenings centred around the cross and in the garden, that the truth about God and God's ways in the world are uniquely and powerfully revealed. Here, Christians believe, reality is focused with a peculiar sharpness and intensity, God's self is made known in new and unexpected ways, and the truth about the human condition is laid bare. Here is the heart of Christian life and believing.

And here, in these strange events, the Christian hope is rooted and grounded. By the miracle of the Easter event God gives the pledge of the restoration of meaning and wholeness to a broken world, a suffering people, and gives the glorious foretaste and assurance of this restoration in the appearance of the risen one. By the raising of Jesus from the dead, God calls all Christians to walk in this same resurrection hope, to follow in the path of Christ which leads from passion through death and burial to the disclosure of life and a birth to newness.

This call to resurrection hope is uttered by the gospel to all situations of human suffering, misery, forlornness and death. In the acute particularity of suffering there is yet a common human experience of agony, wounding and loss, of the stripping of life and hope and future, terminating in a death of self, whether this death be physical or at some other level of the human personality. The audacity of the Christian gospel is its proclamation that just here, at the very point of loss, of death, of burial of life and hope, the miracle of recreation and renewal can begin. At the very heart of the experience of stripping and losing, the seed of new life is sown:

> Is it not strange of all this emptiness,
> The depth of hopelessness,
> That the last emptiness,
> Should mean the height of hope?[1]

This startling and staggering assurance of new life

emerging from death is proclaimed, exemplified and experienced in the Easter event of Christ's rising from the dead. It is in raising Jesus from the grave that God proclaims decisively the divine way of working in the world, a way that takes human loss, failure, darkness and despair, and makes it the very place of healing and hope. It is because Christ himself has taken this road, has shown the way of walking in it, and has borne the full brunt of its cost in his own body on the tree, that Christians see this as the pattern of God's working everywhere, and the pattern for their own lives. Christ is the exemplar, the guarantee and the sign of God's re-creative activity at work in the world.

Yet this central event of the gospel, the miracle of resurrection, also enables the Christian to perceive the same miracle of regeneration constantly in process everywhere in the natural order, in human lives and community, in the whole created cosmos. We dare to believe that everywhere God is at work bringing new life out of death, hope out of despair, light out of darkness, because we have heard and believed the gospel story of resurrection. In the light of that story we can see the signs of God's continuing re-creative love wherever we look, if our eyes are open and our hearts are trusting.

Perhaps one of the clearest signs of this process of regeneration at work in creation is given in the turning of the seasons, the death of the natural world in darkness, cold and barrenness moving to the emergent freshness and beauty of a new season of growth, light and life. There is an ancient Christian tradition which sees profound parallels between the death and resurrection of Christ and the death and rebirth of the natural world in the cycle of the seasons. This tradition itself has its roots in ancient pagan wisdom. It is not only Christians who read the perpetual turning of the seasons as the assurance of continuity and restoration of life. The rise of sap, the lengthening of days and the quickening pulse of growth after long months of darkness and fallow ground have been celebrated from ancient times as the token and guarantee of life and fertility, and even secular twentieth-century urban dwellers may find themselves lifted and energized by this yearly impulse to life in the natural order.

Nevertheless, the cycle of the seasons has a peculiar and profound symbolic significance for Christians, precisely because we cannot divorce the one pattern of death and rebirth in the created cosmos from the other pattern of death and rebirth in the story of Jesus Christ. The re-creative energy of love at work in the turning of the seasons and the bringing of beauty out of barrenness in the natural world is the same re-creative energy of love which effects the miracle of the resurrection. The God who restores life to his beloved son is the God who restores life to his beloved world. As Brother Ramon has written:

The God who created the universe and who indwells every created thing is not a different God from the Father of our Lord Jesus Christ who reveals himself to us in the great prophetic tradition, culminating in the story of Jesus. The God of creation is the God of redemption, and every movement of the created order, the changing of the seasons, the variation of mood, the rhythm and pattern of the world, all these bear witness to the dynamic movement of God's providence and love . . . The pulse of the world is the heartbeat of God, and the dynamic presence of the living God is immanent in his creation. In him we live, move and have our being; from him we come and to him we go. Creation is the dance, the rhythm, the harmony of God, and earth, sea and sky are caught up in the revelation of his love.[2]

Because "creation is the dance, the rhythm, the harmony of God", we see the signs of God's creative and redemptive activity in a special way in the natural world. Luci Shaw expresses this ancient insight with startling vividness in her poem, "The Omnipresence":

> God. His print is everywhere,
> stamped on the macro- and the microcosm.
> Feathers, shells, stars, cells speak
> his diversity. The multiplicity of
> leaf and light says God. Wind,
> sensed but unseen, breathes the old
> metaphor again. Seasons are his
> signature. The double helix
> spells his spiral name.[3]

At least in the northern hemisphere, the Church in its liturgy makes deliberate play on this parallel unfolding pattern of the seasons to illuminate and deepen the celebration of the unfolding pattern of events in the Jesus story. We await the birth of Christ in the coldest, darkest part of the year's turning and welcome the coming of light at the height of the triumph of darkness. We move through Lent and Holy Week in the world's slow awakening from darkness

and winter, when creation itself seems to reach out
for release and birthing. We come to the triumphant
celebration of Easter in spring's glorious outburst of
life and colour, growth and song. We experience
a profound sense of "fittingness" in these liturgical
seasons.

If the movement of the seasons is a sign to the
Christian of God's re-creative work in raising Christ
from the dead, it is also a sign of what God can and
will do in our own lives. The new life bursting out
from the death of the created cosmos is a token of
the new life God can wrest out of the brokenness
and death of human lives. The very tree of shame
has burst into blossom by the miracle of the resurrection, and henceforth

> all trees on earth partake this miracle,
> proclaim this glory.

God's people can thus dare to hope that God will
perform the same recreative miracle of love in our
own lives, and can see the signs of this wherever
they look in the created world:

> Look long, then, here, at this
> budding of dead wood:
> and in our lives,
> however dry or gnarled the grain,
> he'll cause the flower of love
> to sprout again.[4]

The gospels are full of stories of such changed and
raised lives. Those who recognize God at work in
Jesus and respond to the divine invitation to be
transformed find themselves called out of their old

comfortable or desperate lives into risky but liberating and creative newness. The one story of the death and resurrection of Jesus himself may be a more dramatic and intense realization of the transformative power of love, but it is not essentially discontinuous from those other "smaller resurrections" which are scattered throughout the gospel pages: stories of healings, of release from painful memories and past destructive ways of living, stories of deliverance from bondage and oppression, of lavish and liberating love for Jesus, stories of raising from death itself. And in our own lives and situations, we could witness to many other such resurrection stories, in which the Easter experience is relived and re-enacted in fresh times and places and the liberating love of God is revealed in countless ordinary lives.

This, then, is the good news of Easter – nothing less than the conviction that in raising Christ from the dead, God has given the pledge of ceaselessly working for the transformation of all people and all that is in the world into the likeness of the glorified and risen Christ. The challenge of Easter is the call to consent to this resurrection process in our own lives. The risen Christ is the "first-born", the "first-fruits", of this Eastering process, as Paul puts it, but the regenerative power of love unleashed on the first Easter morning does not remain locked into that short span of time and history; it reaches backwards into the past, and forwards into the future, capturing all of space and time in the compass of the original Easter miracle.

To believe in the risen Christ, then, is to consent to this Eastering process, to consent to the Eastering Spirit, in our own lives, in our own world. It is to consent to the passage of death in order that resurrection life may be released. It is to consent to the passing of the old so that the new may be born. Such consent is costly, risky and painful, as Jesus himself and numberless others have shown throughout history, by their faithful obedience to their calling, the setting of their faces towards their own Jerusalem, the surrender of their lives into the hands of their accusers, their willingness to endure the apparent destruction of their life's work and certainties, letting go of what is safe and known and launching out into the dangerous realms of the unknown. Yet the resurrection is the sign that precisely here, at the point of costly consent, a new and undreamt of possibility can take root, new life and hope can be unleashed. Because Christ and countless others before and after him have trodden this way of consent and made it the fruitful path to life, the gospel proclaims with confidence that wherever there is mortal agony, wherever there is groaning and travail in the creation, there the Eastering Spirit is close at hand and at work, offering the possibility of renewal and release into life to those who will consent to the dying of the old and the birthing of the new.

The concept and design of the anthology

The Easter experience, I have suggested, is the very heartbeat and the essential rhythm of Christian faith. Yet, precisely because of its centrality to Christian faith and its familiarity to Christian people, it is all too easy for the extraordinary significance and compelling vitality of the Easter events to become dulled and lost. The gospel narratives of the passion, death and resurrection of Christ are well-known to us, so that we fail to be moved and grasped by their staggering proclamation. Academic debates about the historicity of the original Easter events frequently fail to touch the springs of our thinking, imagination and action. The Church's liturgy, too, is for many people a barrier, rather than a bridge, to renewal in the realities of the Easter faith. Complacent over-familiarity, on the one hand, and alienating incongruity, on the other, bar many from the vital truths which symbol, ritual and word seek to enact and proclaim.

We are constantly in need of a renewed vision of the simple yet profound realities which lie at the heart of our faith. We need eyes opened for seeing, ears unstopped for hearing, a kindled imagination which stirs the heart to response and the will to action. The purpose of this anthology is to create a fresh focus on the Easter events by bringing together a range of poetry and prose readings, set in a particular narrative structure and arranged around a central dominant image, in the hope of provoking such a renewed vision of faith.

The anthology traces the Easter events of resurrection out of death and burial through the imagery of growth in the natural world and the movement of the seasons. It uses images of new life emerging from the soil, of the transformation of winter into spring, of what Hildegard of Bingen calls *viriditas* or greening power, "earth's lush greening", the germinating force which comes from God and permeates all creation.[5] It uses images of the unfolding of flowers, plants and trees from the darkness and hiddenness of seed, bulb and root working underground. These images are brought together to express and interpret the movement of Christian faith from the despair and bleakness of the death and burial of Christ to the glorious miracle of the resurrection, in which God's suffering Son is vindicated and our own lives are raised to newness again. The images used are sensual, earthy, physical; and it is right that they should be so. For if resurrection means anything at all, it is about raised and transformed human bodies and human, bodily lives, the presence of God in our fleshly mortal condition. The sheer physicality and sensuality of the natural seasonal imagery can help us to grasp this bodily reality of the Easter hope. It can also help us to recognize the wider implications of the Easter events for the whole created cosmos. Christ's resurrection is good news, not only for the human condition, but for the wider universe of the entire natural order. The natural images employed in the anthology may encourage us to take seriously the cosmic dimension of the Easter hope and to acknowledge the rightful claim of the earth to share in the fruits of Christ's redemptive work.

Whilst this natural seasonal imagery provides the dominant metaphor for the selected readings, the anthology also has a very particular *narrative* focus and structure. The passage from death to life traced in the Easter story and the movement of the seasons does not take place in universal abstraction, but in a particular time and place, in real human lives and community. The anthology locates the Easter experience in two particular stories, which are placed alongside each other and which merge and mesh together to suggest the personal and narrative focus of the resurrection encounter.

The first narrative is the Johannine gospel story of the death, burial and resurrection of Jesus, told through the eyes and experience of Mary Magdalene. Mary accompanies her beloved friend and saviour to the bitter end of his journey towards death, endures the terrible ordeal of watching him die an agonizing death on the cross, and knows her own life and hope utterly crushed, ended. Refusing to abandon the lifeless body, she comes to the garden of Christ's burial early on the Sunday morning to mourn her Lord's departure and to anoint his body one final time. Beyond all hope and believing, she is wakened and transformed into joy by the garden's secret, and is sent out to share her resurrection healing with others, to proclaim the secret of the garden to those whose lives are broken and devoid of hope as hers had been.

The second narrative placed alongside this first one is the very different story of orphan Mary Lennox's discovery and tending of the secret garden in Frances Hodgson Burnett's children's classic of that name. Mary comes to Misslethwaite Manor after the death of her parents, bereft and lonely and unloved, to be looked after by Mr Craven, her reclusive and embittered guardian uncle. Left to her own devices, she wanders round the huge empty house and out in the vast expanses of gardens. As she does so, she discovers the locked and forbidden garden where, ten years earlier, Mr Craven's wife had been killed. In the discovery, the watching and the tending of the wild, secret garden, this Mary, too, is wakened into life, transformed from "the most disagreeable-looking child ever seen" into a reflection of the radiance and beauty of the garden. The transformation in Mary is completed and reflected in the healing which takes place in the lives of all whom she invites into the garden to share in her secret of discovery and growth.

The two stories, for all their obvious differences, are both Easter stories, celebrating the passage of death to resurrection and the transforming power of love. Both stories trace the painful process of growth through loss and mourning and brokenness to restored life and hope and wholeness. Both stories begin in death and burial, and end in resurrection and proclamation. Both stories have to do with the healing of buried wounds and denied past, and with the energizing impulse of love to restore and reclaim broken lives. Both stories have to do with the cost and risk and consent of renewal, with the abandonment of the past and openness towards the future. Both stories have to do with the journey towards mature and authentic selfhood, a selfhood characterized by integration, independence, freedom and growth, as well as by generous and open relationships with others. Both stories are stories of resurrection discovery, resurrection encounter, resurrection commission.

Nor is it accidental that, in both stories, resurrection discovery, encounter and commission are first and foremost experienced by those who are wounded and vulnerable, by those who are displaced, dispossessed and despised. The child and the woman have much in common. Both are deeply wounded characters, broken and stripped by the loss of love and the death of hope. Both are vulnerable and powerless characters, unrecognized and denied a rightful voice by those who wield power in the societies of which they are a part. Both are displaced and dispossessed characters, the outsiders, uprooted from home and past, belonging nowhere. Both are despised characters, marked by failure and painful past, scorned and ignored by others. It is to these, the wounded, displaced outsiders, the woman and the child, that the gift and miracle of resurrection are granted and the task of proclamation is entrusted.

This feature of the two stories has radical personal and political implications. At a personal level, the woman and the child invite us to recognize and welcome the displaced and dispossessed parts of our own lives which we all too frequently ignore. The outsider is the symbol of the wounded and rejected inner self who cries out for recognition and who bears rich gifts of healing and wisdom in her hands, if we can but welcome and accept her. At a political level, the woman and the child invite us to recognize and welcome the displaced and dispossessed persons within our own communities whom we all too frequently ignore or reject. The outsider is the symbol of the wounded and rejected people in our world who cry out for recognition and who also bear rich gifts of healing and wisdom for our world. If we are sensitive to the radical implications of the two Mary stories, we will recognize the gospel challenge to allow the outsider in.

The resurrection discovery, encounter and commission are experienced by the two Marys when they are welcomed inside the walls of a garden. In the anthology, the image of the garden provides the link between the two Mary narratives and the seasonal imagery, and has significance in a number of ways. In the first place, the garden is a mundane, homely image to which all can relate, but which still has profound personal significance for many as the place where they feel most in touch with themselves, with the earth, and perhaps, too, with that which is more than themselves, whether they name it God or not. In an increasingly industrialized and urban society, where many live in huge, sprawling cities, the garden has become a vital green and open space within the concrete jungle. Here people can still experience the elemental energy of earth's rhythms and the pull of the seasons. It is thus a fitting image, still, of the place where resurrection can be experienced in contemporary lives. Agnes Sanford speaks simply and movingly of the power of the earth to connect us to ourselves and to God:

> The simplest and oldest way in which God manifests himself is not through people but through and in the earth itself. And he still speaks to us through the earth and the sea, the birds of the air and the little living creatures upon the earth, if we can but quiet ourselves to watch and listen . . . There is comfort to be found in the very earth itself and in the creatures that live upon it . . .
>
> Those who live in the country can wander at will upon the consoling earth; they can lie on the grass in the summertime and immerse themselves in the coolness and the fragrance of it. They can walk beside the still waters and find peace. They can lean over an ancient wooden bridge and watch the dance of a millstream and make no effort to pray or even to think, and a forgotten feeling will begin to move and to dance within their souls . . . Even

those who live in cities can find some park or
garden – perhaps some bit of earth that is their
own.[6]

Secondly, the garden is a powerful image of co-
operation and co-creation between humanity and
the natural world, and between humanity and God.
As Thomas Berry puts it, "gardening is an active par-
ticipation in the deepest mysteries of the universe.
By gardening our children learn that they constitute
with all growing things a single community of life.
They learn to nurture and be nurtured in a universe
that is always precarious but ultimately benign."[7]
The symbol of the garden reminds us that resurrection involves both gift and response, demanding our
acceptance of the sheer miracle of new life freely
given and also our co-operation with God's activity
in the world. The raising of Christ from the dead and
the raising of our own lives to newness are sheer,
gratuitous gift, as much beyond human control and
possession as the emergence of green life from the
soil. And yet, we are not merely passive recipients
of life and gift. We are co-creators with God in the
world. God gives the wind, the rain, the sun, the soil
and the life in the seed, but we are called to clear the
ground, to plant the seed and to tend the crop so that
the miracle of new life can come to fruition and not
be wasted. God raises Christ from the dead, and with
him, our lives from the dust, but we are called to
open our lives to the Eastering Spirit, to work with
God in proclaiming and releasing the Easter miracle
to the world. The image of the garden invites us to
recognize the place of human initiative, activity
and industry, as well as divine gift and grace, in
the creative and redemptive process of Easter.

The garden image has a further theological significance. The Easter garden recalls to mind the Eden garden, the garden of God's original intention for humanity, created to reflect God's glory and for the enjoyment of the entire created order, but soon spoiled by sin. As a result of that sin,

> the garden of Eden became overrun with thorns and briars. The roots of [human] divinity became poisoned, twisted and choked with the brambles of sin, and paradise became a wilderness. In this sad story every man is Adam and every woman Eve, and in [their] alienation from the life of God Adam [and Eve] hide in the garden, afraid and ashamed, under condemnation and judgement, with the roots of bitterness and rebellion bearing fruit in suffering and sin. Paradise becomes Paradise lost, and Adam and Eve become wandering vagrants on the face of the earth, barred from the tree of life and bringing forth according to their kind in rebellion, murder and bloodshed.[8]

But now, the effects of this terrible human falling and failing have been reversed by the one who proves himself to be the perfect, second, Adam. Unlike the first Adam, he does not grasp for equality with God but accepts the divinely ordained limitations of the human condition and lives a whole, full, creative life within their bounds. Unlike the first Adam, he does not abuse the power of divinely granted knowledge but uses it wisely to live in love and communion with others, with God, with the creation. Unlike the first Adam, he does not seek to hold on to his own life blindly, selfishly, fearfully, but gives it up for others and finds that, by thus losing his life, he has truly found it. So, by his life, death and resurrection, this Jesus has restored and renewed the garden of Eden, bringing it back to life from the death and barrenness of winter, nurturing within it once again the life, the harmony, the wholeness, for which it had been created.

It is no coincidence that Christ is both betrayed in a garden and then first appears in risen form in a garden. This is a powerful token of the new creation, the restoration of the glory, splendour and beauty of Paradise once lost and now regained. Christ's resurrection and appearance to Mary is the sign of the healing of that ancient rift of sin which had led to the expulsion from the garden. As Lightfoot comments, "Mary, then, was not wholly mistaken in thinking that he who addressed her . . . was the keeper of the garden. In the obvious sense of the term, and as she used it, she was mistaken; but she also, like Caiaphas and Pilate, spoke more truly than she knew".[9] The risen Christ is the gardener who has reopened the path back to Eden which once was barred by flaming swords. He is the gardener who has uprooted the canker of sin and set Paradise in order once more. He calls us inside the garden walls to live again in communion with God and each other, and in harmony with the natural world, as God had first and always intended.

These, then, are some of the resonances and patterns which lie behind the conception and structure of the anthology. Doubtless some of these suggested meanings will speak more powerfully to individual readers than will others. And doubtless there are many more possible patterns and meanings which readers will discover as they bring their own life experience into play with the life stories of the two Marys and the life cycle of the seasons.

The anthology is divided into three main sections, moving through the transformation of winter into spring in the natural world and the transforming encounter in the garden for the two Marys. Each section begins with an extended prose introduction, and ends with a selection of prayers and meditation exercises.

In the first section, the world is gripped in the icy bands of winter. Everything is frozen and sterile. Christ is buried and Mary Magdalene comes to the tomb, her life bereft of all hope and meaning. Mary Lennox comes from India, fresh from her parents' funeral, to the lonely and rambling Misslethwaite Manor, and wanders, aimless and desolate, in the grounds. The death and barrenness of winter reflect the death of hope and love in the two Marys:

> O never again, it seems, can green things run,
> or sky birds fly,
> or the grass exhale its humming breath
> powdered with pimpernels,
> in this dark lung of winter.[10]

The only human response is to mourn the dead body and to cry for mercy.

In the second section, the first stirrings of life in the garden mirror the stirrings of hope in the human heart and the answering of that hope in the resurrection appearance of Christ. Mary Magdalene returns to the tomb and enters the Easter garden – and finds there her Christ, her self. "To the dead Christ comes the robbed self . . . Mary goes blindly back to the tomb, and finds her self, her home, her name."[11] Mary Lennox at last enters her secret garden, and finds there the signs of new life hidden within the soil, and recognizes them as the secret signs of life and hope within her own wounded, bitter self. In the two Marys, joy is kindled again by the miracle of the garden encounter.

In the final section, the garden is alive with the riotous, passionate beauty of spring, and resurrection joy is celebrated in shouts of triumph and the abandonment of the self to God:

> For lo, the winter is past,
>   the rain is over and gone.
> The flowers appear on the earth,
>   the time of singing has come,
> and the voice of the turtledove
>   is heard in our land.[12]

Mary Magdalene goes out to proclaim the news of the risen Lord to the frightened disciples. Mary Lennox proclaims the secret of the garden to those who have need of its healing, and invites them to come within its walls and share its joy. The abundant glory of the Easter garden spills over into the whole created cosmos and the resurrection gospel is proclaimed to the world:

> Now the green blade riseth from the buried grain,
> wheat that in dark earth many days has lain;
> Love lives again, that with the dead has been:
>   Love is come again,
>   like wheat that springeth green.[13]

1

DEATH IN THE GARDEN

The Burial

Imagine darkness and winter. The ground is cold and hard. The trees are bare, stretching out their arms and waiting. The flowers are buried deep within the womb of the earth. The world weeps, the garden is empty.

We first encounter Mary Lennox at the beginning of *The Secret Garden* in a context surrounded by death. She has travelled from one scene of death to another: from her Indian home where a cholera epidemic has wiped out her entire family and household, to Misslethwaite Manor where her guardian uncle, Archibald Craven, lives the life of a lonely recluse, following the sudden and tragic death of his young wife and the illness of his son Colin.

Bereft of family, home and belongings, Mary travels from India to the big old house in the middle of the Yorkshire moors, and everything around her mirrors the desolation, the destruction, the barren waste and lonely emptiness of her own life: the wild, grey expanse of moorland across which she must travel to reach the Manor, and on which "nothing grows but heather and gorse and broom, and nothing lives but wild ponies and sheep"[1]; the sheets of rain endlessly lashing the carriage windows and the wind "making a singular, wild, low, rushing sound"[2]; above all, Misslethwaite Manor itself, with its "near a hundred rooms, ... most of them shut up and locked"[3], its echoing corridors and ancient pictures and fine old furniture neglected and gathering dust; its acres of desolate parkland and garden, barren, cold and empty of life; its strange, sad, sour and secret inhabitants nurturing some bitter burden of grief which Mary perceives but does not understand; and its one, secret, locked garden, harbouring the heart

of the painful past and sealing the inhabitants of
the Manor in its dark and miserable memories. In
her own person, too, Mary reflects the death she
has experienced, a death of love and of home, the
desolation of not belonging to any one or any place
any more: "she had a little thin face and a little thin
body, thin light hair and a sour expression. Her hair
was yellow, and her face was yellow because she had
been born in India and had always been ill in one
way or another", so that "everybody said she was
the most disagreeable-looking child ever seen".[4]

In this desolate landscape of death, where the
painful past is buried and bitterness fuels the hurt
locked in the garden, there is nothing for Mary to do
but to wander down the nights and days, searching
out the gloomy corridors, wending her way down the
garden paths, seeking out the secret garden where
the heart of the grief – and unknown to Mary, the
key to the healing – is buried. It is a time of walking, of waiting, of searching – yet without hope or
desire. It is a time when desire and longing seem to
be long past possible. Death has taken its toll, the
bodies are buried. There is nothing to accomplish but
the painful passage of mourning. Mary's sad, lonely
forays into the gardens are the ritual outworking of
this mourning. And as she walks, the garden, too,
frozen in the sterility of winter, displays the year's
signs and season of death.

In the much sparser gospel narratives of the passion, death and resurrection of Jesus, we first encounter Mary Magdalene, too, in a context surrounded by death. From the gospels we know little
about Mary's previous history except that Jesus had
cured her by casting out seven demons from her
(Mark 16:9; Luke 8:2), and that she henceforth

accompanied Jesus on his preaching and healing ministry. Although tradition has conflated the characters of Mary Magdalene, Mary of Bethany and the woman who was a sinner of Luke 7 into one woman, there is no justification for this conflation, and, in particular, no reason to think that Mary Magdalene was a prostitute before she met Jesus. Her only "sin" was sickness, as the poem by Thomas John Carlisle puts it, and Jesus had released her from this past:

> My "sin" was sickness.
> My afflicted mind
> was captured by devils.
> They filled my days with fear
> and nights with frenzy.
> I was impotent
> to cure –
> or to forgive –
> myself.
> And then he came.
> Perhaps he called me Mary.
> So many times since
> he has called me Mary
> I can't remember.
> But I do remember this.
> He called me and recalled me
> to myself
> and made me whole and healthy
> and so marked
> with joy and gratitude
> I cannot do
> enough for him.
> And so I follow
> anywhere he goes
> and I will not deny him.[5]

Mary Magdalene, like Mary Lennox, has travelled many days and miles when we encounter her in the garden of the burial, the scene of death. But, unlike Mary Lennox's journey, this other Mary's journey had started out in joy and in hope and had only lately turned to grief and to mourning as she watched, in cruel and helpless bewilderment, the ignominious death of Jesus on the cross.

Travelling with Jesus and the other disciples from Galilee up to Jerusalem and the festival, there certainly must have been both weariness of mind and body and periods of doubt about Jesus' destination and purpose. Yet there was great joy and hope, too, a mounting joy and hope amongst those who walked with Jesus that here, in truth, was "the one to redeem Israel".[6] And perhaps it is not fanciful to suppose that in Mary there was a joy and hope of peculiar depth and intensity – a deep and wondering joy in the newfound freedom from the prison of her past, a silent and unshakeable hope in the one who had quelled the forces of darkness unleashed against her mind.

And now, she who had been released from her locked prison of fear has watched her own liberator taken captive, bound and lashed to the cross. She who had known healing and life at his hands must watch him scourged, beaten, put to death, those same hands pierced and disfigured. She who had followed him out from the dark, secret places of her hated past into blazing light and open space, must watch him walk the path to his trial and death, must see him blinded by blood and sweat, the light in his eyes fade as darkness and thunder covered the hill. She who had felt the weight of endless days and nights of madness lifted by his

command, must watch him stagger and fall under
the weight of the cross, reel as the cloud of evil and
despair pressed down on his shoulders. She who had
found in him her home, her self, the blessed welcome
and knowledge of love, must see him betrayed by his
friends, banished from the ranks of his people, must
hear him cry out in uncomprehending dereliction to
his Father, "My God, my God, why hast thou forsak-
en me?"[7] She who had been to him intimate friend,
companion, confidant, trusted and loved by Jesus,
must now stand by helpless and useless, unable to
offer anything but the powerlessness of her simply
being there, watching it all happen to him. He who
had become her saviour, her joy, her life, her healing, her friend, is now abandoned to death, and she
is powerless to save him from his fate or to offer any
sign of consolation. Mary's agony defies description
as she waits and watches by the cross while her
beloved is put to death and her own heart is broken,
twice over – once for Jesus' suffering and the end
of all his hopes, once for her own deep grief and
brokenness. It is not the child's grief, piteous but
blind, as Mary Lennox's is; it is the full-bodied
grief of one who has loved and lived deeply, and
whose very reason for living is slashed away in a
moment.

Yet Mary does not run. Unlike the frightened,
faithless men who have fled, the women remain
huddled together for what poor sustenance they
can glean from the body on the hill. Here at the
scene of death, where there is nothing for them to
say or do save wail with grief and reel with the
senseless cruelty of it, they will not leave. Mary
stays and watches. When the last breath has been
breathed, the long, terrible dying is finally ended,

and the body is down from the cross, slumped and disfigured, it is the women who tend him, washing and anointing and wrapping the body with bands and with spices, performing the last rites of love. Then, in the desolate landscape of death, they leave the shrouded body in the tomb to wander and grieve the long night away. Mary goes to mourn for the friend and saviour who can never come again. Death has taken its toll, the body is buried; and with the buried body, her own life lies buried. Never again, she must have thought, can life or healing come. Hope and joy and desire are long since dead. There is nothing to accomplish but the painful ritual mourning.

Yet, for the two Marys, this long and silent passage of mourning is as necessary to their healing as the silent sterility of winter is necessary for spring. It is the essential passage of Easter eve, without which Easter morning cannot come. Unless the body is really dead and buried, there can be no resurrection. It is the long, painful passage of waiting, of senseless grief and mourning, when it seems that life can never hold pleasure again, desire and joy are wiped out forever. It is the bleak "winter of the spirit", as Maria Boulding puts it[8], which all who hope to celebrate Easter must, in some sense, come to know. And even in this frozen landscape of death, where no sign of life or growth can be detected by human eye, underground the soil is working, the freezing cold cracking the earth's pores open for the emergence of new life again. All lies dormant, sleeping the season's sleep of death. Yet in sleeping, the earth is preparing itself, the season is turning: the world is moving towards spring. And in the two Marys, too, life is present, stirring below

– or better, within – their naked grief. The sower tends the land, prepares the ground in winter for the sowing of the seed. The heart sleeps and grieves, and, all unknowing to itself, awaits the word of the one who will call it to rise in life again.

"You wrap up warm an' run out an' play you,"
said Martha. "It'll do you good . . ."

Mary went to the window. There were gardens and paths and big trees, but everything
looked dull and wintry.

"Out? Why should I go out on a day like this?"

"Well, if tha' doesn't go out tha'lt have to
stay in, an' what has tha' got to do?" . . .

Martha found her coat and hat for her and
a pair of stout little boots and she showed her
her way downstairs.

"If tha' goes round that way tha'll come
to th' gardens," she said, pointing to a gate
in a wall of shrubbery. "There's lots o' flowers
in summer-time, but there's nothin' bloomin'
now." She seemed to hesitate a second before
she added, "One of th' gardens is locked up. No
one has been in it for ten years."

"Why?" asked Mary in spite of herself . . .

"Mr Craven had it shut when his wife died
so sudden. He won't let no one go inside. It
was her garden. He locked th' door an' dug a
hole and buried th' key. There's Mrs Medlock's
bell ringing – I must run."

After she was gone Mary turned down the
walk which led to the door in the shrubbery.
She could not help thinking about the garden
which no one had been into for ten years.
She wondered what it would look like and
whether there were any flowers still alive in
it. When she had passed through the shrubbery
gate she found herself in great gardens, with
wide lawns and winding walks with clipped
borders. There were trees, and flowerbeds, and
evergreens clipped into strange shapes, and a

large pool with an old grey fountain in its midst. But the flowerbeds were bare and wintry and the fountain was not playing. This was not the garden which was shut up. How could a garden be shut up? You could always walk into a garden.

She was just thinking this, when she saw that, at the end of the path she was following, there seemed to be a long wall, with ivy growing over it. She was not familiar enough with England to know that she was coming upon the kitchen-gardens where the vegetables and fruit were growing. She went towards the wall and found that there was a green door in the ivy, and that it stood open. This was not the closed garden evidently, and she could go into it.

She went through the door and found that it was a garden with walls all around it and that it was only one of several walled gardens which seemed to open into one another. She saw another open green door, revealing bushes and pathways between beds containing winter vegetables. Fruit-trees were trained flat against the wall, and over some of the beds there were glass frames. The place was bare and ugly enough, Mary thought, as she stood and stared about her. It might be nicer in summer, when things were green, but there was nothing pretty about it now.

Frances Hodgson Burnett[9]

Joseph of Arimathea, who was a disciple of Jesus, but secretly, for fear of the Jews, asked Pilate that he might take away the body of

Jesus, and Pilate gave him leave. So he came
and took away his body. Nicodemus also, who
had at first come to him by night, came bringing
a mixture of myrrh and aloes, about a hundred
pounds' weight. They took the body of Jesus,
and bound it in linen cloths with the spices,
as is the burial custom of the Jews. Now in
the place where he was crucified there was a
garden, and in the garden a new tomb where
no one had ever been laid. So because of the
Jewish day of Preparation, as the tomb was
close at hand, they laid Jesus there.

The women who had come with him from
Galilee followed, and saw the tomb, and how
his body was laid; then they returned, and
prepared spices and ointments. On the sabbath
they rested according to the commandment.

John 19: 38-42; Luke 23: 55-56

At length the worst is o'er, and Thou art laid
    Deep in Thy darksome bed;
All still and cold beneath yon dreary stone
    Thy sacred form is gone;
Around those lips where power and mercy hung,
    The dews of death have clung;
The dull earth o'er Thee, and Thy foes around,
Thou sleep'st a silent corpse, in funeral fetters
    wound.

John Keble[10]

Jesus is dead. She still cannot grasp it. Her
whole life has revolved around him ever since
her healing and absolution. She has followed
him both close to and from afar . . . The last
week in Jerusalem had been a harrowing one.

Each day the menace of a climactic confrontation with the religious authorities loomed larger, the threatening clouds grew darker. She watched her Lord's suffering deepen, well before the final crisis of trial and execution. And this brought out in her a feverish activity – a "being there" with him minute by minute, in spirit even when she could not be physically near him . . .

So, Mary Magdalene has been caught up in a whirl of activity, an activity that is both her response to and her need in the face of Jesus' sufferings. Then the actual trial and death had been a nightmare – did she perhaps act as a messenger, flying from house to house? Was she running around seeking out the place where Jesus was being tried, following him doggedly in the hope of a glimpse, a small opportunity to do something for him in these dark hours? And then came the crucifixion itself – hideous in the extreme, unbearable to watch, and yet she was compelled by love to be there, to look upon the suffering of her loved one, and to enter into it with him, to be near him in loving support, easing a little of his pain by accompanying his mother, offering to her daughterly concern.

And finally the last agony and the last moments of his earthly life, the dying words, the bowing of his head and the yielding of his spirit. Darkness over the earth. The end.

Not quite! There are things still to do – the body to be removed from the cross and transferred to the garden of Joseph of Arimathea. She and other of the women accompany the body, sit over against the sepulchre and watch the sealing of the tomb. There was the rush to complete the preliminary washing of the body in the short while before sunset when the stone would be rolled in front of the tomb. The more elaborate rituals would have to wait until after the Sabbath. Then . . .?? Home? To Mary's house? To Mary the mother of John Mark? We don't know where she and the other women stayed during those hours between sundown on Friday and dawn on that "first day of the week" . . .

The hours of that Sabbath when Jewish law forbad them to return to the tomb to minister the last loving rites upon the body, must have been bleak. Perhaps the women shared together the rich memories they had of Jesus, wept together, consoled one another, comforted the [other] disciples, and made their plans for their early morning visit to the tomb.

For Mary there was still the promise of that last look upon the face of the Lord, a last opportunity to minister to him in practical ways. Probably she had got no further than that in her thinking. She had not faced, at that stage, the loss she would feel once the stone was rolled in front of the tomb finally and permanently.

Margaret Magdalen[11]

How can we rest in the face of death? the
    women cried,
    with the stench of decay on our nostrils?
How rest on the Sabbath?
We shall prepare spices to cover death,

Sweet aromas for the smell of death
While we pray Jesus to put
   his salve on our sight,
   his balm on our wounds,
   his linen robe against our skin.

O healing hand, O son of the God of
   salvation,
   Stay with me.[12]

Anon

If I was jealous, I was also loyal. When they tried him, I was there, outside the palace, hidden in the crowd alongside his mother and the other women. When they scourged him, clothing him in purple and setting a palm in his hand and a crown of thorns upon his head, I did not weep. I knew what the end would be. I could not remove or share his pain, but I witnessed it, when others like Simon Peter denied him and then ran away. Oh, I knew it was safer for me, a common woman whom none in the lofty court of Jerusalem would suspect of being intrigued with a traitor, to remain as close to him as was possible . . . I am no hero. The only virtue I claim for myself is faithfulness. One of the last gifts I could give Jesus was to stand fast while he suffered, to follow his limping progress up the steep hill, to watch as they bound him spreadeagled on to the wooden cross and banged in the long nails, not to faint or cover my face as they raised the cross and tore his flesh.

They hung my husband on a tree of death. They took him from me. I looked at his feet, which I had once smeared with ointment and bathed with tears when they were dusty and blistered, and saw them newly torn. I looked at his body, which I had cradled in my arms and knew as intimately as I knew my own, and saw it exposed and racked. I looked at his head, which I had held between my hands, and saw it bowed in agony. I looked at his face, which I had stroked and kissed, and saw it streaming with blood . . . I wanted to call to him, to awaken him from his trance of pain, but could not. No words came. The rain fell on him and on me, and the ground under the cross was slippery with mud and with blood, and he and I were alone together and I could not speak to him . . .

After the soldiers had pierced his side with a lance, he was declared dead, and we were allowed to take him down. We had to hurry, for it was nearly sunset and the centurion was adamant that the corpse must be buried before nightfall. We were lucky even to get permission to bury him, that he was not thrown like refuse to the dogs scavenging at the bottom of the hill. His mother held him briefly in her lap, while Martha opened the bag she had brought from the apothecary and found a sponge and a small skin of water. We washed the worst of the blood from his face and limbs, and then I took off my mantle and covered him before John and Joseph of Arimathea took him up and bore him away to the rock chamber in Joseph's nearby garden where we had been given permission to bury him. Three soldiers followed us, to ensure that we did not attempt to make away with the

body and practise our own rites of farewell on
it elsewhere. I walked behind John and Joseph
and Nicodemus, in the middle of Martha and
the Lord's mother, holding their hands, and
the soldiers came behind us, mocking at me
for my uncovered head and hair and calling
me all manner of names . . .

We stumbled across the damp garden. The
tomb was at the far end, half hidden by a
fall of greenery. We laid him inside it, on
a raised stone bed, and then I took Martha's
bag and opened it and extracted the oils and
ointments, the myrrh and spices and bandages
I had instructed her to buy. Jesus had teased me
more than once for my skill at massage, my tal-
ent for easing away the pain from a torn muscle
or a stiff neck, calling me doctor and witch and
miracle worker, but always glad of my mini-
strations. For the last time I anointed his feet
. . . I prepared him for burial while the other
women and the three male disciples and the
three soldiers watched, and as I wrapped him
in the sweetsmelling bandages I sang to him, in
silence, my own lament and my own farewell.

The soldiers heaved and groaned. We would
not help them. At last the great stone slab
fell into its grooved place, and they swore
and spat on the ground and then sat down
and settled their backs against it. There was
nothing left for us to do but go. This was
the most terrible moment: leaving him there,
alone, abandoning him there. His mother coun-
selled against my staying in the garden, to
watch over the tomb, for she feared that the
soldiers, who were already busy unstoppering

a skin of wine, might try to do me harm. So
we trailed back after the slow, stooped figure
of Joseph and went into his house as guests to
do our mourning there.

Michele Roberts[13]

Tree without leaf I stand
Bird unfeathered cannot fly
I a beggar weep and cry
Not for coins but for a hand

To beg with. All my leaves are down,
Feathers flown and hand wrenched off
Bird and tree and beggar grown
Nothing on account of love.

Elizabeth Jennings[14]

I have no wit, no words, no tears;
    My heart within me like a stone
Is numbed too much for hopes or fears.
    Look right, look left, I dwell alone;
I lift mine eyes, but dimmed with grief
    No everlasting hills I see;
My life is in the falling leaf:
    O Jesus, quicken me.

My life is like a faded leaf,
    My harvest dwindled to a husk:
Truly my life is void and brief
    And tedious in the barren dusk;
My life is like a frozen thing,
    No bud nor greenness can I see;
Yet rise it shall – the sap of Spring:
    O Jesus, rise in me.

My life is like a broken bowl,
   A broken bowl that cannot hold
One drop of water for my soul
   Or cordial in the searching cold:
Cast in the fire the perished thing;
   Melt and remould it, till it be
A royal cup for Him, my King:
   O Jesus, drink of me.

Christina Rossetti[15]

It is foolish to minimize death . . . Death causes
infinite pain, despair, anguish; it threatens us,
it dispossesses us . . . Death is absolute void,
loss, penalty, dreary powerlessness; we are radically at the end, the possibility of acting for
ourselves is really and finally closed to us.
Death is the event of the most radical spoilation
and unmastering of our humanity . . .

Ievan Ellis[16]

Who will take away
Carry away sorrow,
Bear away grief?

Stream wash away
Float away sorrow,
Flow away, bear away
Wear away sorrow,
Carry away grief.

Mists hide away
Shroud my sorrow,

Cover the mountains,
Overcloud remembrance,
Hide away grief.

Earth take away
Make away sorrow,
Bury the lark's bones
Under the turf.
Bury my grief.

Black crow tear away
Rend away sorrow,
Talon and beak
Pluck out the heart
And the nerves of pain,
Tear away grief.

Sun take away
Melt away sorrow,
Dew lies grey,
Rain hangs on the grass,
Sun dry tears.

Sleep take away
Make away sorrow,
Take away the time,
Fade away place,
Carry me away
From the world of my sorrow.

Song sigh away
Breathe away sorrow,
Words tell away,
Spell away sorrow,
Charm away grief.

Kathleen Raine[17]

Month of the dead elm,
  the bare thorn.
Only the stormcock delights in dusks
that whip in nights wild with the last gales
  of winter,
and cold mornings to follow.

We see flowers bruised in the mud,
  and the cold-footed people pray for your death.
                    Neil Vivian Bartlett[18]

No night could be darker than this night,
no cold so cold,
as the blood snaps like a wire,
and the heart's sap stills,
and the year seems defeated.

O never again, it seems, can green things run,
or sky birds fly,
or the grass exhale its humming breath
powdered with pimpernels,
From this dark lung of winter.
                    Laurie Lee[19]

Cold is an ugly, painful element in human experience. It is a threat to life. Birds and small animals may die in winter; so do many people living near the starvation line . . . For the rest of us cold may not be a threat in that sense, but it does lower our level of life, reducing us to misery, to preoccupation with our elemental needs, and to a marked reluctance to act in any imaginative, unselfish or constructive way . . . We share in some way in the general frozenness, sterility and apparent death of nature

. . . The earth sleeps, holding its seeds in trust, waiting. The trees sleep, preparing for the great work of spring and summer, for flowering and fruit-bearing.

Maria Boulding[20]

"Why did Mr Craven hate the garden?" Mary said . . .

"Art tha' thinkin' about that garden yet? she said. "I knew tha' would. That was just the way with me when I first heard about it."

"Why did he hate it?" Mary persisted.

Martha tucked her feet under her and made herself quite comfortable. "Listen to th' wind wutherin' round the house," she said. "You could bare stand up on the moor if you was out on it tonight."

Mary did not know what "wutherin' " meant until she listened, and then she understood. It must mean that hollow, shuddering sort of roar which rushed round and round the house, as if the giant no one could see were buffeting it and beating at the walls and windows to try to break in . . . "But why did he hate it so?" she asked, after she had listened. She intended to know if Martha did.

Then Martha gave up her store of knowledge . . .

"It was Mrs Craven's garden that she had made when first they were married an' she just loved it, an' they used to tend the flowers themselves. An' none o' th' gardeners was ever let to go in. Him an' her used to go in an' shut th' door an' stay there hours an' hours, readin' an' talkin'. An' she was just a bit of a girl an'

there was an old tree with a branch bent like
a seat on it. An' she made roses grow over it
an' she used to sit there. But one day when she
was sittin' there th' branch broke an' she fell
on th' ground an' was hurt so bad that next
day she died. Th' doctors thought he'd go out
o' his mind an' die too. That's why he hates
it. No one's ever gone in since, an' he won't
let anyone talk about it."

Mary did not ask any more questions. She
looked at the fire and listened to the wind
"wutherin' ". It seemed to be "wutherin' "
louder than ever.

Frances Hodgson Burnett[21]

Love heeds no more the sighing of the wind
Against the perfect flowers: thy garden's close
Is grown a wilderness, where none shall find
One strayed, last petal of one last year's rose.

O bright, bright hair! O mouth like a ripe fruit!
Can famine be so high to harvesting?
Love, that was songful, with a broken lute
In grass of graveyards goeth murmuring.

Let the wind blow against the perfect flowers,
And all thy garden change and glow with spring:
Love is grown blind with no more count of hours
No part in seed-time nor in harvesting.

Ernest Dawson[22]

Stripling body
that will never grow again
smashed distorted sudden
without pain
silent breathless still.
    Slain.

Felled in a flash.
Lights flashing.
  Sorrow fell.

Sapling body
bowed swift,
truncated seedless
limbs lifeless lying,
leaves still
a memory
bursting full
potentially mature
with promise,
leaves other saplings
growing on
potentially mature
with seed for sowing . . .

What promise they?
When shall their felling be?
How shall it fall?
Sudden swift unready?
Shall they be
upright tall
full grown towards the Infinite,
seed sown (pure strain)
with fruit a hundredfold?
Or stunted twisted weeping
following the wind
and at the felling
left behind
all promise spent
and fruitless seed?

                    Brenda Norton[23]

Who has believed what we have heard?
  And to whom has the arm of the Lord
    been revealed?
For he grew up before him like a young plant,
  and like a root out of dry ground;
he had no form or comeliness that we should
  look at him,
  and no beauty that we should desire him . . .
By oppression and judgement he was taken
    away;
  and as for his generation, who considered
that he was cut off out of the land of the
    living,
  stricken for the transgression of my people?
And they made his grave with the wicked
  and with a rich man in his death,
although he had done no violence,
  and there was no deceit in his mouth.
                   Isaiah 53: 1-2, 8-9

      Here is a pit
      hollowed with the
      harrowing of hate
      it is deep deep
      for falling
      it is dark dark
      for losing
      it is death death
      for growing

      till Christ forge the way
      show the foot-holds down
      marked by his decending feet

Here is a ladder
wrung with tears
it is steep steep
for slipping
it is sharp sharp
for wounding
it is hard hard
for climbing

no guide but Christ

take the ladder down
ask no way but
where the steps are marked
hope no end but
where the feet have gone
think no help but
what the way has forged

take the journey down
take the ladder down

and

Here is a tomb
hammered with the
last lights of love
it is hard as stone
for breaking
is is sharp as flint
for razing
it is sealed sealed
for keeping

till Christ cleft the rock
sear the sealed grave
stride his way seize his own

loose the holds of hell

follow down:
the pit is here
the ladder prayer
the tomb a womb
wherein his life
may rise
but seek no birth:
no seed will sprout
but in the dark of death

Nicola Slee[24]

He descended into the earth.
He had to go on descending
into the deepest experience of death,
entering the place of furthest separation
    from God
until he could descend no further.

It was not easy for the disciples
to believe in the transformation
that was being accomplished.
They knew only that the body of Jesus
was broken and dead.
And they saw that their hearts and their unity
were also in pieces:
    Judas has committed suicide;
    Peter is hiding in shame and remorse;
    two of the disciples,
        judging the reports of women
        that Jesus has been seen alive
        as obviously hysterical,
    break from the group and leave for Emmaus.
All of them are crushed by despair.

Their wonderful dream has exploded.
It is all over.
Finished . . .

Everything is broken, even more cruelly than
before –
>   the body of Jesus,
>   their dreams,
>   their hearts,
>   their power,
>   the body of their unity;
>   all is broken.
And all this brokenness seems only to reveal
their own inner decay and despair,
the inconsolable cry of loneliness,
the horror and emptiness of death.

Jean Vanier[25]

Wrapped in his shroud of wax, his swoon of
    wounds,
still as a winter's star he lies with death.

Still as a winter's lake his stark limbs lock
the pains that run in stabbing frosts about him.

Star in the lake, grey spark beneath the ice,
candle of love snuffed in its whitened flesh,

I, too, lie bound within your dawn of cold
while on my breath the serpent mortal moans.

O serpent in the egg, become a rod,
crack the stone shell that holds his light in
    coil.

O grief within the serpent sink your root
and bear the flower for which our forked
　　tongues wail.

Cold in this hope our mortal eyes forgather
wandering like moths about the tomb's shut
　　mouth;

Waiting the word the riven rock shall utter,
waiting the dawn to fly its bird of god.

Laurie Lee[26]

Thou goest home this night to thy home of winter,
To thy home of autumn, of spring, and of summer;
Thou goest home this night to thy perpetual home,
To thine eternal bed, to thine eternal slumber.

　Sleep thou, sleep, and away with thy sorrow,
　Sleep thou, sleep, and away with thy sorrow,
　Sleep thou, sleep, and away with thy sorrow;
　Sleep, thou beloved, in the Rock of the fold.

Sleep this night in the breast of thy Mother,
Sleep, thou beloved, while she herself soothes thee;
Sleep thou this night on the Virgin's arm,
Sleep, thou beloved, while she herself kisses thee.

The great sleep of Jesus, the surpassing sleep of Jesus,
The sleep of Jesus' wound, the sleep of Jesus' grief,
The young sleep of Jesus, the restoring sleep of Jesus,
The sleep of the kiss of Jesus of peace and of glory . . .

　Sleep, O sleep in the calm of all calm,
　Sleep, O sleep in the guidance of guidance,
　Sleep, O sleep in the love of all loves;
　　Sleep, O beloved, in the Lord of life,
　　Sleep, O beloved, in the God of life!

Traditional Celtic[27]

The symbol of the entombed Jesus, pale and
silent in his winding sheet, is . . . evocative

and . . . immediately contemporary, because
ours seems to be the era of the silent Christ,
the inarticulate Christ, the Christ who grips our
imagination but who will not explain himself.
The helpless Christ seems made for our times,
the Christ of the silent tomb. Many of us are
puzzled by the complexity of the evils that confront us in the world, and paralysed by our own
private frailties. And Christ is often advertised
as a miracle worker, as a political and personal
messiah. Let him into the situation, some say,
whether it be the struggle between nations or
the struggle in our lives, and he will bring
peace. That's what the disciples wanted, it is
what we want and it is what some preach, but
it does not seem to be true for everyone. Many
of the ones closest to him seem to be the most
afflicted. In my own experience, the men and
women who have ministered to me the most
effectively have been flawed characters, often
tragic in their moral frailty, desperate for Christ
to deliver them from their fears and compul-
sions, but their Christ has been the Christ of
the silent tomb. He just waits, and so do they.
They wait down the years for some lifting of
the burden, and it usually does not come. As
they say, they learn to live with it . . .

For many their Christ is the Christ of the
tomb, the waiting Christ, the silent Christ.
And many of them learn to wait, find an
answer in the waiting, and see that the waiting is not an empty thing; it is not an absence
of something, it is a more powerful kind of
presence. Like Paul whose "thorn in the flesh"
was not removed, the waiting is the way they

know God, whose strength is made perfect in weakness. After a while they no longer wait impatiently for something to happen, because the waiting is the happening, it is the way they follow Christ, the waiting becomes the way.

Richard Holloway[28]

Where is the song now
   when all is silent
   and the grey clouds
   mock the sun
   and the husk is empty and dry?
Where is the bright joy
   when the bird on the wing
   is snared
   and ice settles on the water?

How may I travel
   the winter solstice
   when the blood slows
   and the heart quivers
   and is silent?
   Will you in the shroud
   and the dead leaf
   show me a new beginning
   the kingdom and the crown
   in the darkness?

Margaret Torrie[29]

Winter sleeps heavily in the spirit;
Eyes are windows to the glacial land;
Fog curls into the valleys of decision;
No way forward: Where is God
In the winter of the soul?

Faces smile and flash content
But like sparkling snow cover
The dirty slush of despair.
In silhouetted barren branches:
Nothing growing, nothing resting . . .
  emptiness.

Where is God in the winter of the soul?
Will icelogged rivers of love flow again;
Will warmth burn away the cold?
Believing in things unseen:
Hope
  is the winter name of God . . .

                            Sally Dyck[30]

So it's a bad winter, set in
just when hopes had started – late
autumn flowers. Colour frozen out,
excitement shrivelled at the edges.

Night after night two sparrows
have roosted in the outhouse
yards apart, no flutter response
to my torch beam, their heads withdrawn
into a fragile warmth.

So slight a hold on life, their margin
economy! Every day
they go early after food, returning late.
Down to essentials now, with luck
they will survive.
           We can scarcely believe
we shall survive these grey-long days,
the cold, a seeming absence of love.
Love – is it buried under the snow?

Frozen for ever into the ground?

But no, listen! Even on this coldest day,
day of the worst news, I have seen
beneath the privet hedge the slim shoot
of a daffodil spired straight
as a cathedral into the iron air.

And where the snow has given way
islands of grass show green.
The grass is always green, renewed,
continuing.
        Soon the sparrow
cocky feathered will stir about
singing again and fuss and fight and find a mate.

Love one another. It is not too late.
          Michael Marais[31]

In the lives of those who believe and pray,
there are bleak winters of the spirit . . . God
brings us to these winters, these dreary times
of deadness and emptiness of spirit, as truly as
he brings winter after autumn, as a necessary
step towards next spring. But while we are in
them they feel like a real absence of God, or
our absence from him:

   How like a winter hath my absence been
   From thee, the pleasures of the fleeting year!
   What freezings have I felt, what dark
      days seem!
   What old December's bareness every-
      where! . . .

Looking back, you know that these times brought you closer to the Lord of the winter, that it was necessary for you to go through them. In the winters of your prayer, when there seems to be nothing but darkness and a situation of general frozenness, hold on, wait for God. He will come.

Maria Boulding[32]

In the afternoon . . . she ventured into the garden to get a breath of the cold blustery air . . . Winter held sway. The chestnut trees were bare now, in the avenue, and the dead leaves of the beech hedge rustled dryly in the wind. The skeletons of dead plants rattled together like castanets, and the matted ivy on the old wall flapped up and down like a loose curtain.

The stone was as grey as the November sky above it. In the distance, the girl could see the dun-coloured meadows of winter and the faraway smudge of woods. The grey coldness seemed to echo her own life just now. Would she ever know light and warmth, colour and excitement again? Would this desolation last for ever?

She was tired of struggling, tired of keeping up a bright front . . . If only something, however insignificant, would happen to give her hope.

"Miss Read" [33]

Winter seems to me to be a time of death and gloom – even the trees feel my despair, they are lank and dreary. On a wet day there is no escape from its chillness and the fire in the grate will not burn properly. The windows rattle and the draught makes the curtains shiver a little.

Only yesterday I saw a robin perched in the hedge, singing with all his heart, his red breast puffed with the effort of singing and keeping warm . . . My days of despair pass like the winter. I wait for warmer times – for laughter, to feel good again, for fêtes and sunshine, for flowers and fruit from the garden. Pain and sorrow were harder to bear when I saw them to be enemies. Both winter and sorrow are eventually followed by laughter and summer. So I will wait.

Maggie Durran[34]

Death, she thought . . . What had been growing and full of sap, sprouting and erect, taking over the world, had been overcome and was shrivelling back within itself, there was mould and corruption and fading, things dried and fell, and were gradually blotted up by the moisture from the earth. There had been spring and there would be winter. But then spring again. Death and a new life. She could feel both within herself, as though the old blood was drying out, and giving way to new, though the process had hardly begun. It was change, and she could only let it overtake her, without knowing what might be to come, what emotions and beliefs and experiences would replace those of the past. But they could only grow up out of the soil of that past. So everything had been necessary.

Susan Hill[35]

Spring is a promise
in the closed fist
of a long winter. All
we have got is a raw
slant of light at a low
angle, a rising river
of wind, and an icy rain
that drowns out green
in a tide of mud. It is
the daily postponement
that disillusions. (Once
again the performance
has been cancelled by
the management.) We live
on legends of old
springs. Each evening
brings only remote
possibilities of
renewal: "Maybe
tomorrow." But the
evening and the morning
are the umpteenth day
and the God of sunlit
Eden still looks
on the weather
and calls it good.

Luci Shaw[36]

The way of the crucified is the way of joy
in sorrow. Christ is the wounded healer, the
dying life-giver, the man of sorrows in whom
we rejoice. We cannot understand his death
and his wait in the tomb. It wrings our heart,
compels us to gaze at the unbearable face of evil
– a nailed hand, a child's shoe in the middle of

the street in the wake of a speeding car, the
ditch at Babi Yar, the tokens, the wounds of
the Christ crucified until the end of time. And
as we listen and gaze, the sorrow not a whit
diminished, a wild hope rises in us, something
answers from within, and from beyond tragedy,
beyond the tomb, beyond hell itself we hear the
great promise of the Christ of sorrow and of joy:
"Ye now therefore have sorrow, but I will see
you again and your hearts will rejoice, and your
joy no one will take from you."

Richard Holloway[37]

. . . Winter is the season of our growth:
creation held in quiet suspense,
pausing for fresh breath
and new endeavour;
when bulbs build up resources for their life
and searching roots reserve their strength,
looking to the rhythm of another year;
when stem and flower fall broken to the ground
and seeming loss is richer gain
as earth receives its food
to rise again next year.

Winter is neither death
nor even slumber.
Winter is the season of our growth.

Donald Hilton[38]

Bewildering as it all seems at the time, it
is actually in the darkness that most of our
growing is done. The rule in the natural world
– growth in the darkness of the soil, growth in
the darkness of the womb – applies to the spiritual too . . .

It is painful, of course, as it was for Mary Magdalene. In facing the darkness, sometimes prolonged periods of it, we should acknowledge the pain, allow it to *be* pain and not seek to call it by other names. We need to admit that it is not easy.

> There is no consolation. There is no relief. There is no hope certain; the whole system is a mere illusion. I, who hope so much, and am so rapt up in the soul, know full well that there is no certainty. The tomb cries aloud to us – its dead silence presses on the drum of the ear like thunder, saying, "Look at this, and erase your illusions."

We may well share this sense of hopelessness and illusion. To continue at all requires courage, big-heartedness and the generosity that Ignatius stressed so much . . . Of one thing we can be certain. God will not be outdone in generosity. He calls us to enter the darkness in order to discover him in new ways, in order to grow. We cannot see, we do not feel, we no longer know but, as St Bernard assures us, "God can never be sought in vain, not even when he cannot be found."

Margaret Magdalen[39]

[Christ] has penetrated into the depths of
    darkness,
loneliness, rejection, agony and fear,
in order to touch the depths of darkness
in each one of us

and to call us to belief,
to call us to walk in this world of darkness,
loneliness, rejection, agony and fear –
hoping, trusting in the resurrection . . .

[So] do not turn aside from your own pain,
your anguish and brokenness,
your loneliness and emptiness,
by pretending you are strong.
Go within yourself.
Go down the ladder of your own being
until you discover –
like a seed
buried in the broken, ploughed earth
of your own vulnerability –
the presence of Jesus,
the light shining in the darkness.

Jean Vanier[40]

Christ's work, both in the church and in the hearts of Christians, often goeth backward that it may go the better forward. As seed roots in the ground in the winter time, but after comes better up, and the harder the winter the more flourishing the spring, so we learn to stand by falls, and get strength by weakness discovered – we take deeper root by shaking . . . Such is the goodness of our sweet Saviour, that he delighteth still to show his strength in our weakness.

Richard Sibbes[41]

Why should I start at the plough of my Lord, that maketh deep furrows on my soul? I know that he is no idle husbandman, he purposeth a

crop. O that this white, withered lea-ground
were made fertile to bear a crop for him, by
whom it is so painfully dressed; and that this
fallow-ground were broken up!

Samuel Rutherford[42]

There is nothing more that they can do
   For all their rage and boast;
Caiaphas with his blaspheming crew,
   Herod with his host,

Pontius Pilate in his Judgement-hall
   Judging their Judge and his,
Or he who led them all and passed them all,
   Arch-Judas with his kiss.

The sepulchre made sure with ponderous stone,
   Seal that same stone, O priest;
It may be thou shalt block the holy One
   From rising in the east.

God Almighty, He can break a seal
   And roll away a stone,
Can grind the proud in dust who would not
     kneel,
   And crush the mighty one . . .

There is nothing more that they can do
   For all their passionate care,
Those who sit in dust, the blessed few,
   And weep and rend their hair:

Peter, Thomas, Mary Magdalene.
   The Virgin unreproved,
Joseph, with Nicodemus, foremost men,
   And John the well-beloved,

Lay Him in the garden-rock to rest;

Rest you the Sabbath length:
The Sun that went down crimson in the west
    Shall rise renewed in strength.

God Almighty shall give joy for pain,
    Shall comfort him who grieves:
Lo! He with joy shall doubtless come again,
    And with Him bring His sheaves.

Christina Rossetti[43]

The winter cold
has not yet left my bones.
I shiver in this birthing Spring's
first light.
No sun, no shadow,
only the truth
of tree and slated sky.
Though no bird sings,
with certitude I brace
against the failing chill,
awaiting Easter.

Myrna Reid Grant[44]

For there is hope for a tree,
    if it be cut down, that it will sprout again,
    and that its shoots will not cease.
Though its root grow old in the earth,
    and its stump die in the ground,
yet at the scent of water it will bud
    and put forth branches like a young plant.

Job 14: 7-9

PRAYERS

God of all our growing,
take our roots down deep
in the long, dark winter season
  of our grief.
Nurture the resurrection life in us,
in the secret places of the soil,
in the barren, frozen earth, underground,
  where no eye can see.
Send your Spirit where the cold season rages
  and speak to us the promise of spring.

Nicola Slee

When the winter of my life
  Threatens me with pain and death,
Leave me not in loneliness
  To its cold and icy breath;
Breathe upon me from above
  And enfold me in your love.

Brother Ramon[45]

How long wilt thou be absent? – for ever?
Oh, Lord! Hast thou forgotten to be gracious,
and hast thou shut up thy loving kindness in
displeasure? Wilt thou be no more entreated? Is
thy mercy clean gone for ever, and thy promise
come utterly to an end for evermore? Why dost
thou make so long tarrying? Shall I despair of
thy mercy? Oh God! far be that from me; I am

thy workmanship, created in Christ Jesus; give
me grace therefore to tarry thy leisure, and
patiently to bear thy works, assuredly knowing, that as thou canst, so thou wilt deliver me,
when it shall please thee, nothing doubting or
mistrusting thy goodness towards me; for thou
knowest better what is good for me than I do;
therefore do with me in all things what thou
wilt, and plague me what way thou wilt.

Lady Jane Grey[46]

We pray to you, O Promised One, and ask
what hope have you to give us when heaviness
weighs on us like a blanket and our hearts can
find small cause for joy? What promise can you
make that would restore our spirit? We see need
on every side, hear questions without answers,
feel hunger with no food that satisfies. How
long, O God, before you come? How long before
you once more work wonders in our hearts and
land? We have need of you. We go blind for lack
of hope. Come quickly, Promise of our God.

Janet Schaffran and Pat Kozak[47]

Praise to you for summer, fall and spring
But faith reserves the right to wonder
When chill of winter invades our bones.

Where are you when a sign is asked
And none is given,
And barrenness in earth and soul
is all we know?

Enough of it! We've had enough
of grey and cold and emptiness.
life wears heavily and joy becomes a victim,

in the winter of our hearts.

What good is death if Easter never comes,
If any sign of risen life is only in our memory
and promises are all past due?

Revive. Restore. Lift up our hearts
and with them, all creation.
Breathe upon your world and warm us all.

What word have you for those who wait,
For those who long like deer for running
     streams,
Like infants for their mothers' breasts,
Who yearn like birds for flight?
What word have you for we who wait?
            Janet Schaffran and Pat Kozak[48]

God of the sealed tomb,
we cannot bear to leave
your dead and buried body.
But you send us away
to mark the long night
of our mourning without you.
You lie in death alone,
beyond the bounds of our feeble knowing.

Numbed by our grief and sorrow,
we cannot interpret you:
you have gone far from us,
down into darkness,
deep into death.

In your great love,
wait for us
where we grieve in the darkness,
till we return to the grave

to find you,
risen, released in the night.

Nicola Slee

O God, it is your will that we should be bap-
tised into the death of your Son our Saviour;
give us true repentance that we may pass with
him through the grave and gate of death, and
be reborn to new life in joy, through him who
died, was buried and who rose for us, Jesus our
Lord.

Taizé Collect[49]

Blessed be God
   for all the little deaths that I have died:
   for the accident which taught me the frailty
     of my flesh,
   for the operation which faced me with my
     mortality,
   for the broken love-affair which turned my
     heart to stone,
   for the bereavement which emptied my life
     of meaning.

Blessed be God
   for each beginning of a resurrection:
   for the discovery of the strength of the spirit
     in this flesh,
   for the awareness of undying love holding me
     firmly,
   for the re-kindling of a new and purified love,
   for the revelation of a universe filled with the
     Glory of God.

Blessed be God for all the little deaths that I
   have died,

Blessed be God for each beginning of a resurrection.
Blessed be God for all whose hands were raised
to wound me,
Blessed be God for all who shared in resurrecting
me.

In dying and in being resurrected I face the future.
I will not shut my heart against the crushing
load of the world's sin and sorrow.
Christ will bear me up.
I will not turn away from the one who wounds
me,
Christ will heal us both.
I will embrace that which kills me,
Christ uses it to bring me home.

Blessed be God for resurrection and for life.

Anon[50]

O God who brought us to birth,
and in whose arms we die,
in our grief and shock
contain and comfort us;
embrace us with your love,
give us hope in our confusion,
and grace to let go into new life,
through Jesus Christ, Amen.

Janet Morley[51]

Blessed be God for the faithfulness of Mary,
who endured the wounding and stripping
of her beloved on the tree,
who kept watch on this long and bitter night
while his body lay in the tomb

and her own life lay buried there.

In her faithfulness we find courage to keep
    faith.
In her loneliness we gain strength to stand
    alone.
In her brokenness we know the recognition
        of our marred and broken lives.

Make us faithful like Mary,
    when faith is stripped down
        to the night of Easter Eve,
Until we come at last
    to share in the full glory
        of Resurrection Day.

Nicola Slee

EXERCISES

1   "Mr Craven had the garden shut when his wife died so sudden. He won't let no one go inside" (p.46). It is a natural human response to pain to seek to bury and deny it. Think of the occasions when people try to bury and deny their hurts. What are the reasons for this human reaction? Have the readings in this section stirred any memories of past or more immediate hurts for you? Use the following guided meditation[52] to relive the memory and ask Christ's healing for it.

Relax in the presence of Christ who sees the past and wants to heal its effects. Ask Christ to help you see the past as he sees it and have it healed at his pace and in his way.

Next, pinpoint the hurt. *What* causes you pain about this event? What do you wish had happened differently? What would it take to have everything feel perfect? What is the worst that could happen? *Whom* do you blame for the pain? Who do you fear, avoid, judge harshly, because of this event? If you could change anybody, who would it be? Draw a large seed on a sheet of paper, and inside the seed describe briefly the painful experience. Thank God for so much growth potential.

Tell Christ how you feel hurt. Ask Christ's help to reconstruct that scene until you relive the way you felt. Have Christ enter the scene. What does he do and say to you?

Ask Christ's help in living out his reaction. What one thing will you do to live out the healing and forgiveness God has brought you? Write this along the outside of the seed to remind yourself of what will release the seed's potential growth.

Finally, pray Psalm 103 (or some other psalm or passage of thanksgiving for healing), thanking God for the ways you are loved.

2   "If I was jealous, I was also loyal" (p.51). According to the biblical narratives, it was the small band of women who remained faithful to Jesus at the crucifixion and the burial, while the male disciples (all but John) fled. Why do you think this was? How do you imagine the women felt as they followed Jesus up the hill to the place of execution, endured his death and then prepared his body for burial? Did they want to escape from it all? What kept them there? Try writing a journal account of the events of these few days from the perspective of one of the women. Become aware of the feelings of pain, grief, hopelessness and anger which this exercise sparks off in you, as well as any feelings of strength, persistence and power. Recognize and name these strengths and weaknesses in yourself, and write them down.

3   "This was the most terrible moment: leaving him there, alone, abandoning him there" (p. 53). Why is this moment so hard for Mary? What does she feel at this point as she walks away from the body laid in the tomb? Reconstruct the scene in your imagination. In what ways do you experience the challenge to "let go" and "walk away"

in your own life? What is God calling you to abandon at this stage of your journey? How do you feel about this? What do you want to say to God? What is the reply?

4   "We share in some way in the general frozenness, sterility and apparent death of nature" (p.57). When and how do you experience "frozenness, sterility and apparent death"? Are such times related to the cycle of the seasons for you? Or to other cycles and patterns in your life? How do you cope with such periods? "How may I travel/ the winter solstice/ when the blood slows/ and the heart quivers/ and is silent" (p.67)? Are there any signs in your own experience that "winter is the season of our growth" (p.73)?

Think of a time or situation in your own experience which appears to be particularly barren, sterile and fruitless; a situation in which you feel blocked, empty, uncreative or powerless – perhaps a particular relationship, or an aspect of your work, lifestyle or prayer. Try drawing or painting the experience, finding a visual symbol which represents the way it feels to you. Don't think about what you will draw too much beforehand, but trust your intuition. Afterwards, reflect on what you have drawn. What do you see? Do you see any signs of hope or growth in the situation? Or is it a situation you are being called to let go and let "die" in some sense?

5   "In the lives of those who believe and pray there are bleak winters of the spirit" (p.69). How are we to respond to such times? How are we to

pray when we do not feel or experience God's presence? Does Jesus' experience of passion and death help us to make sense of such times? And the experience of Mary Magdalene?

6 "Looking back, you know that these times brought you closer to the Lord of the winter" (p.70). Try to identify the ways in which your own experiences of bleakness, loss and suffering, of whatever kind, have given you gifts of insight and understanding or brought you closer to God. How was Christ present in these times?

Think of one particular event or situation in your life which felt very bleak and difficult at the time, but which you now recognize to have been a time of important growth. On a piece of paper, make three columns. Head the first one "an experience through which I have grown" and jot down words or phrases which describe how the experience felt at the time. Head the second column "losses" and write down the losses you experienced through this situation, things you had to give up or which were taken from you. Head the third column "growth and gain" and write down the strengths and insights you have derived from the experience. Now thank God for the growth which has come out of this past difficult time. If there are still aspects of this time which remain painful and unhealed, think how these can be offered to God for healing and further growth. You may like to use the healing meditation in number 1 above.

7 Make a study of the burial narratives in the gospels, using commentaries and the passages in the anthology. You could also collect and

study artists' depictions of Christ being taken down from the cross and buried in the tomb. These might be used as the basis for a display in your home or church during Holy Week.

8   During Lent, create and tend an Easter garden as a sign of the good news of resurrection in your local environment. This might take the form of a conventional Easter garden in church, but it could take other forms. A small corner of a garden, a row of window boxes or tubs, or an unused piece of waste ground might be transformed with bulbs, seeds and plants. Or some wall space in your local church, school or workplace might be used to mount a display, which could be changed as Lent progresses, beginning with images of bleakness and barrenness and moving towards growth and life. Natural images could be placed alongside images from the passion story and images from local life in the community.

9   Keep a Lenten journal and try to trace the patterns and signs of your own growth during this period. You might include reflections on some of the passages in the anthology which speak most powerfully to you, or make your own collection of readings for Lent. Newspaper cuttings, pictures and postcards can be added.

2

LIFE STIRS IN THE GARDEN

Mary Comes to the Tomb

Imagine the first hint of newness, the first breath of spring which, no sooner has it whispered its message to the earth than it is gone. A faint breeze stirs across the sleeping world, the fingers of an uncertain sun touch tiny, tight buds and slowly warm the watching, waiting earth. The world hopes, the garden is waking.

As she explores the empty, wintry landscape of Misslethwaite Manor, something begins to change in Mary. Slowly, imperceptibly, a strange new summons to life is stirring within her, born of the curiosity kindled by Martha's tale of the locked and secret garden. Hardly aware of her longing or understanding her curiosity, Mary begins to seek out the garden. She finds herself constantly walking in the Manor grounds, searching down the pathways, scanning the walls and the trailing ivy for a sign of the hidden gateway, all the time wondering and imagining what the secret garden might be like. And, as she wanders endlessly in the silent grounds and empty pathways, the bracing, bitter cold begins to shock her into life and thought, the strange currents and smells blown off the dry, brackeny moor begin to work their own fertile magic on Mary's mind and senses. "Living, as it were, all by herself in a house with a hundred mysteriously closed rooms and having nothing whatever to do to amuse herself, had set her inactive brain to work and was actually awakening her imagination. There is no doubt that the fresh, strong, pure air from the moor had a great deal to do with it. Just as it had given her an appetite, and fighting with the wind had stirred her blood, so the same things had stirred her mind. In India she had always been too hot and languid and weak to care much about anything, but in this place she was beginning to care and to want to do new things. Already she felt less 'contrary', though she did not know why."[1] The season's turning towards newness and creativity is beginning to work a similar transformation in Mary. Mind, body, sense and imagination are each called into life and activity by the stirring to life in the natural world around her.

Even as she walks and is herself wakened, Mary's walking in the places of buried past and pain is itself a kind of waking of the past to newness again. It is as if, in her walking down the corridors and the paths and the gardens, she is calling them to life again, opening doors and memories and places to the quickening movement of life pulsing in the wind, in the earth and the sun. She is waking her new world with her, calling it out of darkness and forgetfulness, inviting it to respond to the possibility of healing.

Mary's awakened curiosity does not remain unrewarded for long. First, the robin whom she has encountered on her explorations leads her to the flowerbed where she finds the key to the garden. Then, looking and searching anew, it is the robin again who shows her the way into the garden, who leads her to the locked door hidden underneath the trailing ivy. In mounting excitement and sudden, breathless wonder, Mary turns the key, pushes back the door, and stands inside the secret garden.

For Mary Magdalene, enduring the long, hard night of mourning, we cannot imagine any such corresponding quickening to hope and life. Mary's life and self are, it seems, irretrievably lost, gone for ever. Yet, even now, at the bitter end of Mary's journey, in the bleak winter of her loss, there is a dark, black, restless longing and yearning, a constant turning in her thoughts and in her tears and in her steps back to the place where her beloved lies. She will not abandon the beloved, abandoned body. To the desolate landscape of death where her love and her life lie buried, Mary must return. To the garden of mourning she must come again, wandering in the early daylight, seeking again her Lord, coming, hope against all hope, desire against all reason, half crazed with the longing of love which has no other desire than to be with the beloved, to keep dumb watch where no other duty can be performed.

She comes to the garden, but she finds his body gone, disappeared, stolen. Distraught and overwhelmed by the sudden loss of the body she desperately yearns to be near, she rushes out from the tomb, frantically seeking him still, like the lover of the Song of Songs, endlessly searching, searching but not finding:

> I sought him whom my soul loves;
> I sought him, but found him not;
> I called him, but he gave no answer . . .
> "I will seek him whom my soul loves."
> I sought him but found him not . . .
> "Have you seen him whom my soul loves?"[2]

Yet, for this Mary, too, the longing and the seeking are not long unrewarded. Against all hope, against all reason and expectation, Mary meets her beloved in the garden, and encounters in the place of death her living Lord. In the timeless, speechless, sudden, sharp moment of meeting, of calling, of naming and recognition, Mary is restored to herself and to life, in a moment welcomed, known, healed, held, renewed, restored. Going back to the tomb, back to the place of desolation, she finds "her self, her home, her name".[3]

For both Marys, there is an essential quality of stillness, as well as of great joy, in the garden encounter. It is a meeting, a finding, which goes beyond speech, to touch and welcome some hidden source of pain into recognition, acceptance, forgiveness and healing. For Mary Lennox, the encounter in the secret garden is an encounter not only with the locked and buried past of Misslethwaite Manor, but with her own locked and wounded self. As she looks, first in stillness and wondering silence, at the wild garden trailing brown rose creepers and swaying tendrils from the branches, then walks quietly around the flowerbeds searching out signs of life in the grass-covered beds, she is seeking some essential sign of hope within herself too, a sign which shows that all is not dead within her own self and life, that growing quietly and deeply within her are the seeds of life. She greets the "sharp little pale green points . . . sticking up out of the black earth"[4] with a quiet, rapturous joy deeper than laughter; it is a recognition of the burgeoning life in Mary, a welcome to the new thing that is growing there, mirrored in the garden.

And for Mary Magdalene, too, the encounter with the risen Lord is at the same time an encounter with herself. As she turns towards the gardener in her bewilderment and grief, the Lord welcomes her and greets her with her name. In the moment of recognition, there is the full restoration of Mary's broken selfhood, the acceptance of all that she is and has been, the transformation of the wounded past into the springs of life and hope again. Mary's response in the one uttered word, "Rabboni!", is, like the other Mary's, quick and rapturous, too deep for further speech, full-hearted and unhesitating. She, too, recognizes in the encounter, not only her friend returned in life from the tomb, but also her own restored and quickening self, the life in her welcomed, accepted, healed and renewed.

Yet there is loss and even a kind of death, too, in the garden encounter. For Mary Lennox, the wild, secret garden shows all the signs of its ten years' neglect. The unkempt, unruly disorder mirrors the neglect in Mary's own life, demanding recognition and acceptance before renewal can begin. For Mary Magdalene the loss is sharper and deeper just as the encounter with the risen Lord is the more miraculous and sweeter than Mary Lennox's discovery. At the same time as Mary is restored to her beloved Christ, and he gives her in abundance the assurance of joy and hope, there is, too, a harsh note of demand and relinquishment. Mary is not to touch or cling to the raised Christ. She must let go, she must relinquish the beloved, familiar, physical presence so that she may know him in his wider presence in his people and his world, and so that she may know herself more deeply, more truly, more freely. At the heart of the resurrection encounter Mary experiences separation and loss, as well as reunion and gain. The risen Christ is restored to Mary, and Mary is restored to herself, but the old pattern of relationship between them is broken, and Jesus demands a new level of trust, responsibility and independence in Mary. The Lord invites her to a new knowledge and faith in him, one which does not depend on sight or touch or physical proximity, but on a deeper trust and the relinquishment of old, familiar ties so that the new may be known. It is a costly and painful lesson for Mary to learn in the midst of her joy.

For the two Marys, the still, quiet moment of encounter in the garden is the essential moment of their healing. It is the first moment of Easter, the first hour of dawn on resurrection day. It is a moment which combines ecstasy and pain, recognition and consent, reunion and separation, discovery and loss. It is a moment of gift and demand, a turning away from the old and towards the new. It is the first day of spring, when it is possible to give thanks out of a true heart for the passage of winter, and when it is time to turn from grief and mourning to the new life which stirs within.

Mary felt lonelier than ever . . . . She went out into the garden as quickly as possible, and the first thing she did was to run round and round the fountain flower garden ten times. She counted the times carefully and when she had finished she felt in better spirits . . . She went into the first kitchen-garden and found Ben Weatherstaff working there with two other gardeners. The change in the weather seemed to have done him good. He spoke to her of his own accord.

"Springtime's coming," he said. "Cannot tha' smell it?"

Mary sniffed and thought she could. "I smell something nice and fresh and damp," she said.

"That's th' good rich earth," he answered, digging away. "It's in a good humour makin' ready to grow things. It's glad when plantin' time comes. It's dull in th' winter when it's got nowt to do. In th' flower gardens out there things will be stirrin' down below in th' dark. Th' sun's warmin' em. You'll see bits o' green spikes stickin' out o' th' black earth after a bit."

"What will they be?" asked Mary.

"Crocuses an' snowdrops an' daffydowndillys. Has tha' never seen them?"

"No. Everything is hot, and wet, and green

after the rains in India," said Mary. "And I think things grow up in a night."

"These won't grow up in a night," said Weatherstaff. "Tha'll have to wait for 'em. They'll poke up a bit higher here, and push out a spike more there, an' uncurl a leaf this day an' another that. You watch 'em."

"I am going to," answered Mary.

Frances Hodgson Burnett[5]

Listen, I am the earth
I cover the whole world over,
Above me is air and ocean
River and lake,
I spread beneath your feet.
You walk on me.
Tread softly.
Seeds planted in me grow
Nourished by the richness of my soil
Their roots burrowing down
Holding firmly to me
As they sway in the breeze
Or the waters flow.
Plants in the air,
Weeds in the water,
I make everything grow.

Anon[6]

The earth is always there, always taken for granted, never remembered, always trodden on by everyone, somewhere we cast and pour out all the refuse, all we don't need. It's there, silent and accepting everything and in a miraculous way making out of all the refuse

new richness in spite of corruption, transforming corruption itself into a power of life
and a new possibility of creativeness, open
to the sunshine, open to the rain, ready to
receive any seed we sow and capable of bringing
thirtyfold, sixtyfold, a hundredfold out of every
seed.

Anthony Bloom[7]

It is dark in the moistened earth
Where the seed for a season lies
Buried down deep as a dry pregnant husk
Till the earth is pushed aside.
Nurtured by warmth, it has waited alone
Till the time to spring up has come
 Then the rest in the dark is transfigured
  with light
 As the Spirit works out her plan.

June B. Tillman[8]

The soil, moist, dark, a bed for conception,
receives the seed. Soon new life
is kicking in the belly of Mother Earth.
Salvation's age-old shape repeats . . .

Eugene H. Peterson[9]

One of the nice little gusts of wind rushed
down the walk, and it was a stronger one
than the rest. It was strong enough to wave
the branches of the trees, and it was more
than strong enough to sway the trailing sprays
of untrimmed ivy hanging from the wall . . .
Suddenly the gust of wind swung aside some
loose ivy trails, and more suddenly still Mary

jumped towards it and caught it in her hand. This she did because she had seen something under it – a round knob which had been covered by the leaves hanging over it. It was the knob of a door.

She put her hands under the leaves and began to pull and push them aside. Thick as the ivy hung, it nearly all was a loose and swinging curtain, though some had crept over wood and iron. Mary's heart began to thump and her hands to shake a little in her delight and excitement. The robin kept singing and twittering away and tilting his head on one side, as if he were as excited as she was. What was this under her hands which was square and made of iron and which her fingers found a hole in?

It was the lock of the door which had been closed ten years, and she put her hand in her pocket, drew out the key, and found it fitted the keyhole. She put the key in and turned it. It took two hands to do it, but it did turn.

And then she took a long breath and looked behind her up the long walk to see if anyone was coming. No one was coming. No one ever did come, it seemed, and she took another long breath, because she could not help it, and she held back the swinging curtain of ivy and pushed back the door which opened slowly – slowly.

Then she slipped through it, and shut it behind her, and stood with her back against it, looking about her and breathing quite fast with excitement, and wonder, and delight.

She was standing *inside* the secret garden.

Frances Hodgson Burnett[10]

Now on the first day of the week Mary Magdalene came to the tomb early, while it was still dark, and saw that the stone had been taken away from the tomb. So she ran, and went to Simon Peter and the other disciple, the one whom Jesus loved, and said to them, "They have taken the Lord out of the tomb, and we do not know where they have laid him."

John 20: 1-2

On the morning of the third day I resolved to avoid sleep and evil dreams by leaving the bed I shared with Martha and going out. Better to walk, exhausted, than to sleep and be tortured. I drank some water, and splashed my face and hands, and then slunk out of Joseph's house, sliding the bolt of the garden door very gently so that I would not wake the others. It was very early, and the servants were not yet up. The light was blue, paling towards a grey dawn, and I could see well enough once my eyes grew accustomed to the dimness. It was the hour of changing light, the hour when the night transforms itself into the day, the hour, so my mother used to tell me when I was a little girl, the spirits of the dead walk abroad. I shivered, for the air was chilly and wet with the dew falling, and I was glad of the big, rough cloak lent to me by Joseph's maid. I was barefoot, for in the darkness inside the sleeping house I had not been able to find my sandals, and so I crept forwards over the fresh grass which felt wonderfully wet and soothing to the soles of my feet.

I knew where I was going. There was only one place to go. Some Jews practise veneration of the dead bodies of holy men, watching over them and honouring them and praying by them, but I believe I was driven by need alone, my own selfish need to be near him. If I hide in the bushes beside the tomb, I thought, the soldiers will not see me, and I shall be able to be near my Lord and this will perhaps soothe my grief.

At that moment I had a clear memory of his body, pierced and bleeding as he hung on the cross . . . I stood still, gripped by a burning pain that flowed and then ebbed, leaving me hollow and wasted, like a place of cold ashes inside, and beat my fists against my forehead in despair. I spoke to the pain severely, I willed it to depart. So, having prayed for a few moments, I moved on.

The tomb formed the end of a twisting path planted on each side with cypresses. As I came to the last bend in the path, I hesitated and looked about, unsure which was the safest way to go, whether to make my roundabout approach by plunging into the bushes beyond the cypress trees to the right or to the left. And then, standing puzzled and sorrowful on the stony path, my eyes still sore from crying and my head aching from lack of sleep, the dew and the drizzle dampening the cloak I had drawn forwards to cover my head and my face, I felt fear leave me, and guilt too. If I were a mourner, I would go to him straight and not by a devious way. I did not have to act the penitent and skulk up ashamed. I hugged myself

with my strong arms, and then I straightened
my aching back and walked quickly around the
last bend in the path and so up to the tomb.

It was empty. The stone blocking the en-
trance had been rolled back, and the soldiers
had vanished, and when I peered into the
darkness inside I saw the raised stone bed
blank and empty, the body gone and the grave
clothes tumbled upon it.

Michele Roberts[11]

On the first day of the week Mary Magdalene cometh early. She who is supremely the
forgiven sinner, whose heart is utterly given to
her Saviour, is the first to go, when the Sabbath
is over, to be near by that body of which she has
twice already anointed the feet, and to which
she would now aid in giving the last care of
love . . . She comes early – while it is still dark.
But the dawn is already breaking, and she can
see that something has happened; the mouth
of the tomb, which had been closed by a great
stone, is open . . . She does not look further;
she jumps to two conclusions – first that the
body of the Lord is no longer in the tomb, and
secondly that this is because his enemies have
stolen it. At once she turns and . . . runs first
to Peter and to that other disciple who was
known as the most intimate . . . Her message
is not what she had seen, but the inference she
had drawn; in her dismay she is so sure that she
states it as a definite fact: "They came and took
the Lord out of the tomb and we do not know
where they put him." This loving woman, who
had anointed and kissed the feet of the Lord,

identifies him with his body. To remove that
is to remove him . . .

William Temple[12]

The season's anguish, crashing whirlwind, ice,
Have passed, and cleansed the trodden paths
That silent gardeners have strewn with ash.
The iron circles of the sky
Are worn away by tempest;
Yet in this garden there is no more strife:
The Winter's knife is buried in the earth.
Pure music is the cry that tears
The birdless branches in the wind.
No blossom is reborn. The blue
Stare of the pond is blind.

And no-one sees
A restless stranger through the morning stray
Across the sodden lawn, whose eyes
Are tired of weeping, in whose breast
A savage sun consumes its hidden day.

David Gascoyne[13]

It was the sweetest, most mysterious-looking
place anyone could imagine. The high walls
which shut it in were covered with leafless
stems of climbing roses, which were so thick
that they were matted together . . . All the
ground was covered with grass of a wintry
brown, and out of it grew clumps of bushes
which were surely rose-bushes if they were
alive. There were numbers of standard roses
which had so spread their branches that they
were like little trees. There were other trees in
the garden, and one of the things which made

the place look strangest and loveliest was that
climbing roses had run all over them and swung
down long tendrils which made light swaying
curtains, and here and there they had caught at
each other or at a far-reaching branch and had
crept from one tree to another and made lovely bridges of themselves. There were neither
leaves nor roses on them now, and Mary did
not know whether they were dead or alive, but
their thin grey or brown branches and sprays
looked like a sort of hazy mantle spreading
over everything, walls, and trees, and even
brown grass, where they had fallen from their
fastenings and run along the ground. It was
this hazy tangle from tree to tree which made
it look so mysterious. Mary had thought it must
be different from other gardens which had not
been left all by themselves so long; and indeed,
it was different from any other place she had
ever seen in her life.

"How still it is!" she whispered. "How still!"
Then she waited a moment and listened to
the stillness. The robin, who had flown to his
tree-top, was still as all the rest. He did not
even flutter his wings; he sat without stirring,
and looked at Mary.

"No wonder it is still," she whispered again.
"I am the first person who has spoken in here
for ten years."

She moved away from the door, stepping
as softly as if she were afraid of awakening
someone. She was glad that there was grass
under her feet and that her steps made no

sounds. She walked under one of the fairy-like arches between the trees and looked up at the sprays and tendrils which formed them.

"I wonder if they are all quite dead," she said. "Is it all a quite dead garden? I wish it wasn't."

. . . Everything was strange and silent, and she seemed to be hundreds of miles away from anyone, but somehow she did not feel lonely at all. All that troubled her was her wish that she knew whether all the roses were dead, or if perhaps some of them had lived and might put out leaves and buds as the weather got warmer. She did not want it to be a quite dead garden. If it were a quite alive garden, how wonderful it would be, and what thousands of roses would grow on every side?

Frances Hodgson Burnett[14]

. . . all is still; earth is a wintry clod:
But spring-wind, like a dancing psaltress,
   passes
Over its breast to waken it, rare verdure
Buds tenderly upon rough banks, between
The withered tree-roots and the cracks of frost,
Like a smile striving with a wrinkled face;
The grass grows bright, the boughs are swoln
   with blooms
Like chrysalids impatient for the air,
The shining dorrs are busy, beetles run
Along the furrows, ants make their ado;
Above, birds fly up in merry flocks, the lark
Soars up and up, shivering for very joy;
Afar the ocean sleeps; white fishing-gulls
Flit where the strand is purple with its tribe

Of nested limpets; savage creatures seek
Their loves in wood and plain – and God renews
His ancient rapture!

Robert Browning[15]

Frost-locked all the winter,
Seeds, and roots, and stones of fruits,
What shall make their sap ascend
That they may put forth shoots?
Tips of tender green,
Leaf, or blade, or sheath;
Telling of the hidden life
That breaks forth underneath,
Life nursed in its grave by Death.

Blows the thaw-wind pleasantly,
Drips the soaking rain,
By fits looks down the waking sun:
Young grass springs on the plain;
Young leaves clothe early hedgerow trees;
Seeds, and roots, and stones of fruits,
Swoln with sap put forth their shoots;
Curled-headed ferns sprout in the lane;
Birds sing and pair again.

Christina Rossetti[16]

The spring winds awaken the earth and the
rain softens it, making it receptive to the life-
laden seed. Both wind and water are images of
the Spirit, powerfully breathed and abundantly
outpoured to make us receptive to God's seed-
word. As a gardener uses broken down organic
material to enrich the humus, so the Spirit uses
our failure and weakness and our forgiven sin
to build in us a receptive humility. Nothing is

wasted. In the earth of our flesh and our minds, and so in the earth of our planet, God has sown his powerful Word:

As the rain and the snow come down
    from heaven
and do not return there until they have
    watered the earth,
    making it blossom and bear fruit,
and give seed for sowing and bread to eat,
so shall the word which comes
    from my mouth prevail;
    it shall not return to me fruitless
without accomplishing my purpose
    or succeeding in the task I gave it.

Isaiah 55: 10-11

How nearly it might have been "fruitless", smothered by the cold, inert soil; but no, it will *succeed*. Within our very failures God's plan of love is going forward, and will not fail.

Maria Boulding[17]

Into [the] icy winter of sin shines the Sun of Righteousness, and the warmth of his rising dispels the darkness, radiates the earth with the flow of spring, gently melting the snow and ice, and releasing the life-giving waters of the earth. The cold hardness of the ground is softened to enable the new life to spring forth, and the rays of the sun draw out the colour, the fragrance and the beauty of plants and flowers. Springtime is upon us, vitality is within and around us, and we are all caught up

in the cosmic movement of the divine life-force
which is the breathing of the Holy Spirit over
creation:

> When you send forth your Spirit
> they are created,
> and you renew the face of the earth.
> *Brother Ramon*[18]

A seed is a particularly potent symbol. If
you had never observed the processes of nature
before and you were given a tiny seed in the
palm of your hand, you could not possibly guess
the startling form of life that lies hidden within
it. It is a miraculous thing to which only a
hardened heart can fail to respond. Within a
tiny, inert and apparently lifeless speck lies
the potential for new and greater forms of life,
but that potential will never be fulfilled unless
that seed first dies to itself in its present form.
In other words, nature speaks to us endlessly
of that principle of life which we see revealed
and achieved in a totally new way and through
a totally new form in what we call the death
and resurrection of Jesus Christ.

The death of one form is necessary in order
that another, hitherto hidden, form of life may
spring into existence. Jesus was completely
aware of this process at the heart of all true
living. He spoke of his own forthcoming death
precisely in these terms. "Unless a grain of
wheat falls to the ground and dies, it abides
alone. But if it dies, it bears a rich harvest."
He saw his death as a dying to himself in order
that something new and more enduring might

be revealed. What a harvest it has borne. Not only resurrected life as different to the limited life he formerly lived as is a hyacinth to the bulb from which it springs, but also the release of Spirit in the world through which millions upon millions of lives have been reshaped according to the pattern of Christ. The greater part of that harvest is still to come!

. . . If you understand the lesson of the seed, which is death and resurrection, you will look with fresh insight on your own life. You will begin to recognize many moments and situations in which life is not opening up to you and yielding its true harvest because you are trying to preserve life in its present form. It is like a man who insists on keeping a seed in a matchbox and yet wonders why there are no flowers in his garden. You may need to let a particular aspect of your life die to its present form in order that new life may spring from its husk. You must have the courage to bury that seed, whatever it represents, in the dark soil of God's keeping, and to trust Him with it. Soon, very soon, there will be signs of Spring again in your life.

Gary Davies[19]

God's plan for humanity
began like a tiny seed.
In this seed
is contained the magnificence of a huge
    cedar tree,
and within this tiny seed
lies the future of millions of other seeds
which will take form as the tree grows.

In the seed is life,
and all is marvellously programmed within.
As the seed unfolds,
as the child is conceived,
so it begins to grow
and we begin to see its beauty
All that was hidden in the seed
begins to be revealed
as it unfolds.

The fullness of the plan of God
is an unfathomable secret,
known in its entirety only to God.
But each person
in the long, immensely long, line of generations
is able to say "yes" or "no" freely
to the unfolding of this plan –
a very little "yes" or "no" –
but freely said.

Jean Vanier[20]

God dug his seed
into dry dark earth.
After a pushing up
in hopeful birth
and healing bloom
and garland grace
he buried it again
in a darker place

Twice rudely-planted seed,
root, rise in me
and grow your green again,
your fruited tree

Luci Shaw[21]

Mary's skipping-rope had hung over her arm when she came in, and after she had walked about for a while she thought she would skip round the whole garden, stopping when she wanted to look at things. There seemed to have been grass paths here and there, and in one or two corners were alcoves of evergreen with stone seats or all moss-covered flower-urns in them.

As she came near the second of these alcoves she stopped skipping. There had once been a flowerbed in it, and she thought she saw something sticking out of the black earth – some sharp little pale green points. She remembered what Ben Weatherstaff had said, and she knelt down to look at them.

"Yes, they are tiny growing things and they *might* be crocuses or snowdrops or daffodils," she whispered.

She bent very close to them and sniffed the fresh scent of the damp earth. She liked it very much.

"Perhaps there are some other ones coming up in other places," she said. "I will go all over the garden and look."

She did not skip, but walked. She went slowly and kept her eyes on the ground. She looked in the old border-beds and among the grass, and after she had gone round, trying to miss nothing, she had found ever so many more sharp, pale green points, and she had become quite excited again.

"It isn't a quite dead garden," she cried out softly to herself. "Even if the roses are dead, there are other things alive."

Frances Hodgson Burnett[22]

And can these dry bones live?
these bare boughs sprout green?
In my hand the twigs snap –
no sign of living sap –
and each stalk
is sharp, dry as chalk,
scratches blood
with the hard knot of wood.

And can these dry boughs live?
Yes, since one tree of death
bore love's last breath
  (no harder wood
  no bleaker bough
  no sharper thorn
  we'll ever know)
and flamed with the fruit of Christ's risen body
on the first Good Sunday,
all trees on earth partake this miracle,
proclaim this glory.

Look long, then, here, at this
budding of dead wood:

and in our lives,
however dry or gnarled the grain,
he'll cause the flower of love
to sprout again.

Nicola Slee[23]

To turn from the cold and barren winter of sin,
from the darkness and paralysis of a life in the
icy grip of death, and to surrender to the sweet,
warm and fragrant airs of forgiveness, acceptance, reconciliation and love, is the springtime

of the soul. The creative powers of new life are at work, the sap is rising, the tight buds are opening, the air is balmy and inebriating, and the smell of creation is wild and ecstatic. Conversion is the bursting forth of new life, the stirring of the creative powers of love, and the soul cries out in gladness, because creation itself seems wholly new to the eyes of one who has gazed upon the crucified Jesus.

Brother Ramon[24]

Mary stood weeping outside the tomb, and as she wept she stooped to look into the tomb; and she saw two angels in white, sitting where the body of Jesus had lain, one at the head and one at the feet. They said to her, "Woman, why are you weeping?" She said to them, "Because they have taken away my Lord, and I do not know where they have laid him." Saying this, she turned round and saw Jesus standing, but she did not know that it was Jesus. Jesus said to her, "Woman, why are you weeping? Whom do you seek?" Supposing him to be the gardener, she said to him, "Sir, if you have carried him away, tell me where you have laid him, and I will take him away." Jesus said to her, "Mary." She turned and said to him in Hebrew, "Rabboni!" (which means Teacher). Jesus said to her, "Do not hold me, for I have not yet ascended to the Father, but go to my brethren and say to them, I am ascending to my Father and your Father, to my God and your God." Mary Magdalene went and said to the disciples, "I have seen the Lord"; and she told them that he had said these things to her.

John 20: 11-18

See the dust on the path lamely dragging:
No, let her be, Mary moves towards her peace,
Deep calls unto deep, a grave for a grave,
A carcass drawing towards a carcass in that
    unhappy morning;
Three days was this one in a grave, in a
    world that died
  in the cry in the afternoon. It is finished,
The cry that drew blood from her like the
    barb of a sword.

See her, Christ's Niobe, drawing with her
    towards the hill
The rock of her pain from the leaden Easter
Through the dark dawn, through the cold
    dew, through the heavy dust,
To the place where there is a stone that is
    heavier than her torn heart;
Uneasily the awkward feet find their way
    over thorns
With the annoyance of tears doubling the
    mist before her,
And her hands reaching out to him in barren
    grief.

Her moan is as monotonous as a dove's,
Like Orpheus mourning Eurydice
She stands amongst the roses and cries
    without mourning
"They have taken away my Lord, taken him
    away,"
  To disciple and angel the same cry
  "And I know not where they have laid him."
  And to the gardener the same frenzy.

Made wild. Broken. She sank within herself

in her grief.
The understanding reels and reason's out of
     joint, until
He comes and snatches her out of the body
     to crown her –
  Quickly like an Alpine eagle falling on its
     prey –
With the love that moves the stars, the
     power that is a Word
To raise up and make alive: "and he said
     unto her, Mary,
  She turned herself and said unto him,
     Rabboni."

Saunders Lewis[25]

I stood shuddering on the path. Suddenly I
was too hot, my woollen cloak making me
sweat. I threw it off, realizing that I had stood
there stunned for some time, for the drizzle
had stopped and the sun was climbing the sky
and taking with it the glittering wetness from
the grass and bushes and trees. My first clear
thought was that John and Joseph could not
have done it, a young man and an old one to
pit their strength against three brutes of armed
soldiers. We had heard no cry, and no alarm had
sounded. Then I realized that the Romans had
triumphed after all, tricking us into believing
we could bury our Lord ourselves and then
stealing his body back from us under cover
of night. I could not understand their logic,
for, with the Lord's body gone, there would
be plenty to believe him resurrected in the
body and immortal . . . Only great trouble
could come of this. I stilled my questioning

and my useless desire to weep at this fresh loss, even the remains of Jesus gone from me for ever now, and turned round to flee back to the house and wake the others and warn them of the mischief done, the danger to ourselves, the retribution that was sure to follow.

As I turned, I saw a man standing at the bend in the path where I had stood earlier, watching me. He wore a rough woollen robe of the same drab colour as mine borrowed from Joseph's maid, and so I took him for one of the servants, and, when I saw that he held a rush basket filled with figs in one hand, I knew him to be the gardener. I did not stop to think of the folly of admitting to him that I was a witness to the opening of the tomb. I could not resist stepping closer to him and putting out my hand in supplication.

"Tell me, friend," I begged him: "do you know what they have done with the body? Do you know where they went with it?"

He put down his basket and looked at me, and I looked back at him, not having observed his face before this.

"Mary", he said, and stretched out his hand towards mine.

I did not need the scarlet weal on his palm as proof. I knew him.

"Rabboni", I saluted him: "Jesus."

I moved nearer him, so that our hands would have met, except that he stepped back.

"Don't touch me," he said, and then smiled at me, to show that he did not mean his words to hurt.

"Why can't I touch you?" I blurted, not understanding anything.

"I'm here with you now," he said: "and I shall be with you always. I shall never leave you. But I am not in the body as I was before. We cannot love each other now as we did before. You know this already in your heart."

Michele Roberts[26]

To the dead Christ comes the robbed self . . . The hope of the early days is challenged and broken in the cross, the unveiling of the heart's darkness . . . But if hope, mortally wounded, is still capable of turning back to the abandoned body, there is still a discovery to be made . . . Mary, having turned, she, "the one who had turned", again and again, in ever-dwindling hope, now finds that hope answered. Turning, over and again, to the name, the figure, the recollection of Jesus . . . issues at last in knowing with utter clarity that it is still he who calls us into our unique identity . . . Conversion, the turning of *metanoia*, the repentance of which the New Testament speaks, is the refusal to accept that lostness is the final human truth. Like a growing thing beneath the earth, we protest at the darkness and push blindly up in search of light, truth, *home* – the place, the relation where we are not lost, where we can live from deep roots in assurance. Mary goes blindly back to the tomb, and finds her self, her home, her name; her protest, her dissatisfaction with dissatisfaction, is decisively vindicated. Mary is not dead because Jesus is not dead. "I will not leave you desolate. I will come to you.

Yet a little while and the world will see me no more, but you will see me; because I live, you will live also." *John 14: 18-19*

Rowan Williams[27]

Mary Magdalene . . . makes her return to the tomb while it is still dark. If hope seems gone, Mary will still come back seeking the body of Jesus. Mary remembers Jesus as the man who knows her past, and who, in forgiving her, gave her back to herself. For Mary, it is not just the Lord's body, but the Jesus who had loved and affirmed her who has been taken away . . . Her suffering is the pure pain of loss . . . It pierces to the very core of being, to the sense of being loved, being valued and being given meaning . . .

Returning to the empty tomb, Mary went back in memory to her first "turning back". She was remembering her conversion, and again the tears began to flow: tears of compunction in which deep sorrow for sin, longing desire and the passion of love flow together as one. It was the goad of God awakening her to his coming even in his absence, like a spear opening the wound of love. The empty tomb echoed the hollow emptiness of her heart, sensing nothing but the pain of yearning. But . . . she does not go away. She turns back *again* and lingers by the empty tomb. Then she stoops to look into it. But still she weeps, and to the angels' question, "Why are you weeping?" she can only express her experience of loss: "They have taken away my Lord, and I do not know where they have laid him". But, saying this, the evangelist underlines, "she turned round". She turns again, another conversion. Turning round, she sees Jesus as a stranger, the known hidden in the unknown. But she does not give up. Like the lover in the Canticle, she goes on seeking (Cant 3: 1-3). Jesus, appearing as a gardener, adds to the question of the angels his own question, "Whom do you seek?" To weeping in the Passion must be added seeking for the Resurrection. Mary is ready to go on hoping for she knows not what, as she is ready for labour beyond her natural strength. "Sir, if you have taken him away, tell me where you have laid him and I will take him away." She seeks Jesus with the whole of her being. She is, therefore, ready for his coming, and she hears when Jesus speaks her name: "Mary".

Yet again, the evangelist underlines the movement, "she turned". This is a further conversion, simple but total. She addresses him as "Master". All the experience of their past relationship is made present in that word, and in the gesture that seeks to embrace Jesus. The words of the Canticle could be hers: "I have found him whom my soul loves and I will not let him go" (Cant 3:4) . . .

She returns, turns back, turns round, and turning, sees. She asks and seeks. While it was still dark, she draws upon the memory of where Jesus has been for her. She refuses to accept that lostness is the end of the process. Her hope goes beyond hopelessness. Like a blade of grass pushing up beneath heavy concrete, relentlessly she seeks the light. Her faith, her hope and her love are all in the waiting. And in that blind stirring of love, that is becoming a passionate living flame, Resurrection's dawn is silently breaking through the innermost heart of her loss. Mary is not dead because Jesus is not dead.

But the Resurrection is still coming. This is the mystery. There is yet another "turning" for Mary. "Do not cling to me", says Jesus. She was not to cling to the knowing she had of him. There was more yet to come. She is being taken into communion with the Father as Jesus prepares to give her their shared life in the Spirit . . . No longer was Jesus to be simply *with* her in the flesh. The presence of the Spirit of Christ was to be *within* her. Now she must show, in some small way, that she has grasped not just the love story of Jesus and Mary but also the mystery of Jesus *in* Mary. She must, therefore, turn again, turn back to where she had started, and know the place for the first time, because now she knows it new, in God. She must turn back and tell her story, give her "confessions": the memory of the great things God had done in her. She must bear witness, through the story of her own life, to God's saving love in her, and so lead others to run back to Jesus . . .

Mary is prepared to let go of Jesus in the flesh to do what he asked of her, going out into the future. Always we must seek and go beyond where we are, never resting. Now, becomes "Passion" when we are called to go further. There, where he goes before us, is "Resurrection". Resurrection is a symbol of purification from what we can grasp, because God wants to give us more.

Pamela Hayes[28]

"Mary": the answer is her own name, spoken by a voice she knew . . . Her name, so spoken, reaches her heart. She turns to face the speaker. "Rabboni": the cry of devotion accompanies a movement as she hastens to clasp those feet which once she had bathed with tears. So she draws the first declaration of the risen Christ. "Cling not to me, for not yet am I gone up to the Father." The weakness to which such love as Mary's is liable is that it clings too closely to the physical form . . . She must learn to love and trust and serve, even though she can no longer caress his feet or hear his voice proclaim her name. Not to the Lord as he tabernacled in the flesh, subject to all limitations of the body, is she to cling; but to the Lord in his perfect union with the Father.

So he taught her the meaning of that last appearance, the final withdrawal of his physical presence, which we call the Ascension . . . But his Ascension means that he is perfectly united with God; we are with him wherever we are present to God; and that is everywhere and always. Because he is "in heaven" he is everywhere on earth; because he is ascended, he is here now. Our devotion is not to hold us by the empty tomb; it must lift up our hearts to heaven so that we too "in heart and mind thither ascend and with him continually dwell"; it must also send us forth into the world to do his will; and these are not two things, but one.

William Temple[29]

As long as Mary Magdalene and the women still felt the physical nearness of Jesus, they were unshakeable in their faithfulness and perseverance. The one who died, the dead body, the corpse to be anointed and buried, connected them with him. Their cold dismay begins only when they come to the tomb on Easter morning and find that the body of Jesus is no longer there. . .

The encounter between Mary Magdalene and the risen Jesus can only be understood in the light of this special human and personal relationship with Jesus . . . Mary Magdalene, all alone, in tears, hears a voice asking why she is weeping. Believing that it is the gardener, she complains that the body of her Lord has been taken away. Only when Jesus calls her by name, "Mary", does she recognize him and cry out, "My master".

Up to that point everything is understandable, obvious and clear. But then comes the remark which is strange, cold, and rejecting, and which destroys all the feeling of returning happiness: "Don't touch me! I have not yet returned to my Father" . . .

We cannot eliminate the shock which this remark necessarily causes. This is no longer the tender, friendly Jesus. It is no longer possible to touch or anoint his body. He cannot be brought back and held fast. Mary Magdalene may no longer spontaneously throw her arms around him.

The continuity which women seek is broken. The naïveté of childlike faith and trust is over . . .

Mary Magdalene experienced physical salvation in a way which went beyond almost everyone else. She loved Jesus personally. Without him, her life did not seem worth living. She showed tenacity and staying power. She never doubted him. But now she begins to cling to him. It is not the dead Messiah which makes her doubt, but the lost body of Jesus. It is here that she experiences death; here her existence falls apart.

I would prefer to translate the words "Don't touch me" like this: "Grow up, be mature! Accept the grief of parting".

"Why do you seek the living among the dead?" the angel asks the women in the gospel of Luke. It is the same message, and it means, "Where you seek permanence there is only death. Where you are changed, there is life" . . . Spontaneous childlike faith, however firm and permanent it may seem, must change and be submitted to the pain of parting. Only in this way can it grow up and mature . . .

In her encounter with the risen Jesus, Mary experiences the sorrow that the old order passes away, that nothing can be repeated, and that this is the only way in which new things can happen.

Elisabeth Moltmann-Wendel[30]

To the doubting Thomas Jesus said, "Touch me," and to the ecstatic Mary Magdalene, "Touch me not." To the one there was the invitation to cleave to him in faith rather than depend on visible and tangible evidence. To the other there was the invitation to create a space in order to grow in relationship, a call to greet the unexpected, to move on from a dependence on physical presence, from the desire to trap and be trapped in the known and familiar, to deepen in love, to find security in unknowing. Hence the apparent contradiction . . .

We cling fearfully to all that spells security. Yet, as we dare to let go, indeed embrace the dark, we find the Lord we thought we had lost in new and radical ways . . . A clinging in any relationship cramps it, until one or other person feels trapped. When we set each other free and allow one another growing-space, then we learn what it is to "dance" together evolving new patterns for growth. What Mary Magdalene discovered at the mouth of that cavernous tomb – which opened on to the abyss of her horror, the grave of her hopes and memories – we all discover as we pursue with fidelity our calling to prayer. The Lord constantly voids our preconceived expectations, surprises us, comes to us from behind (when we are facing in the wrong direction), gently loosens our fear-filled grip on the known and understood, and goes before – ever before – dancing ahead, touching the earth lightly and lovingly and beckoning us to join him. He will not be bound by grave clothes, or anything else other than love. He calls us on to freedom and joy in a passionate, holistic and holy life . . .

When the grey days come and the "dark nights" of the soul, when our spirits flag and we mourn the loss of former spiritual consolations, this woman with her impetuosity and vigour encourages us to search, to look into the emptiness, to face it squarely, to recognize that once more the Lord has eluded us as we looked for him in the expected place or way. But she points us to a radically new experience of resurrection where the grave of our hopes becomes the gateway to a new dimension of relationship with the Risen Jesus. We dry our tears, turn from our tombs and discover for ourselves the everlasting Easter of the Heart. It is the way of Mary Magdalene – the joyful journey she made from pain to passion, lust to love, fear to faith, doubt to dancing.

Margaret Magdalen[31]

It was as if
The sun were at last returning
To this earth, in slow majesty
Down through the vast space rolling
His ponderous path of flame –
So glows through the morning mists
Beaded with dew, heavy among the trees
The gentle warmth of dawn light,
As if another day could dawn
In this place.
Garden of sepulchres, at the end of the winter
Empty and barren, all that summer brought
Withered and vanished. Emptiness.

Mary, you came through the gate where
    night lingers
Into this sudden stillness, came very slowly
A fluctuating silhouette, trailing through
Tides of mist and the cold dew,
Gripping your frozen spices –
Is it not strange of all this emptiness,

The depth of hopelessness,
  That the last emptiness,
  Should mean the height of hope?
  One bare place in all this barrenness
  Should bring to birth new life
  Beyond expectation?

Let not one cold tear startle your cheek,
Look where the body should have been
And see a promise of Paradise.
Gardener? (Indeed, He sowed
Gethsemane with tears)
Now, see at the touch of this Sun returned
To earth, the garden not with verdure,
Rich with flowers, flowers.

David Middleton[32]

  Mary, weep not, weep no longer,
  Now thy heart hath gained its goal;
  Here, in truth, the Gardener standeth,
  But the Gardener of thy soul,
  Who within thy spirit's garden
  By his love hath made thee whole.

  Now from grief and lamentation
  Lift thy drooping head with cheer;
  While for love of him thou mournest,
  Lo, thy Lord regained is here!
  Fainting for him, thou hast found him,
  All unknown, behold him near!

Philippe de Grève[33]

Rise, daffodil,
against the stones
that shall yield
to your yellow vow.

Rise, onion shoot,
from an odious shroud
to green exclamation;
your death is done!

Rise, children
of the winter mind,
run to the garden –
kneel to the sun.

Barbara Esch Shisler[34]

O risen Lord,
I do not ask you to forgive me now;
There is no need.
I came tonight to speak to your dead body,
To touch it with my hands and say "Forgive,"
For though I knew it could not speak to me
Or even hear, yet it was once yourself;
It is dissolved and risen like a dew,
And now I know,
As dawn forgives the night, as spring the winter,
You have forgiven me. It is enough.
Why do I kneel before your empty tomb?
You are not here, for you are everywhere;
The grass, the trees, the air, the wind, the sky,
Nothing can now refuse to be your home;
Nor I. Lord, live in me and I shall live.

Andrew Young[35]

We sat down together on the grass, and I
listened while he spoke. I put away from myself

as severely as I could my longing to take hold of him, though I knew it would return later with great sorrow and bitterness, and attended to what he said. When he had finished, he stood up, and I with him, and then he raised his hand in blessing and farewell, and was gone. A trace of fragrance of spices and aromatic oil lingered on in the air under the trees. I had no more business there. I turned round and walked steadily back along the path, my face warm and wet with tears, towards the house. But in my heart there began a great beating, the rising and swelling of a joyful and triumphant song: I have seen the Lord. Let all the people rise up and proclaim with me: I have seen the Lord. And so my pace quickened just as the song did, until I was running, careless of the stones that tore my bare feet, and flinging myself in through the doorway of Joseph's house.

Michele Roberts[36]

Where I wander – You!
Where I ponder – You!
Only You, You again, always You!
You! You! You!
When I am gladdened – You!
When I am saddened – You!
Only You, You again, always You!
You! You! You!
You above! You below!
In every trend, at every end,
Only You, You again, always You!
You! You! You!

Levi Yitzchak of Berditchev[37]

PRAYERS

God of all our growing,
call our shoots up from the soil
in the sharp spring season
of our awakening.
Nurture the resurrection life in us,
    in the fragile, burgeoning thrust of green,
    in the delicate bud, the trembling leaf,
    the first, tentative signs of our growth.
Send your Spirit where the new season dances
    and bring us into the promise of spring.

Nicola Slee

Let me seek thee in longing, let me long for
    thee in seeking:
let me find thee in love and love thee in
    finding.

St Anselm[38]

My Lord and God. I do not desire thy Paradise;
I do not desire the bliss of the After World; I
desire only thee thyself.

The Rabbi of Ladi[39]

O God, seek me out of thy mercy that I may
come to thee; and draw me on with thy grace
that I may turn to thee.

O God, I shall never lose all hope of thee even though I disobey thee; and I shall never cease to fear thee even though I obey thee.

O God, the very worlds themselves have driven me unto thee, and my knowledge of thy bounty has brought me to stand before thee.

O God, how shall I be disappointed seeing that thou art my hope; or how shall I be despised seeing that in thee is my trust?

O thou who art veiled in the shrouds of thy glory, so that no eye can perceive thee! O thou who shinest forth in the perfection of thy splendour, so that our hearts have realized thy majesty! How shalt thou be hidden, seeing that thou art ever manifest; or how shalt thou be absent, seeing that thou art ever present, and watchest over us?

Ibn 'Ata' Allah[40]

Almighty God,
whose Son restored Mary Magdalene to
   health of mind and body
and called her to be a witness to his resurrection:
forgive us and heal us by your grace,
that we may serve you in the power of his
   risen life;
who is alive and reigns with you and the Holy
   Spirit, one God, now and for ever.

Alternative Service Book 1980[41]

   Christ our healer,
   beloved and remembered by women,
   speak to the grief which makes us forget,
   and the terror that makes us cling,

and give us back our name;
that we may greet you clearly,
and proclaim your risen life,
Amen.

Janet Morley[42]

No one can put together what has crumbled
    into dust,
but you can restore a conscience turned to
    ashes;
you can restore to its former beauty a soul
    lost and without hope.
With you, there is nothing that cannot be
redeemed;
you are love, you are creator and redeemer;
we praise you, singing: Alleluia!

Gregory Petrov[43]

God of power,
God of people,
You are the life of all
that lives,
energy
that fills the earth,
vitality
that brings to birth,
the impetus
toward making whole
whatever is bruised
or broken.
In You we grow
to know the truth
that sets all creation free.
You are the song

the whole earth sings,
the promise
liberation brings,
now and forever.

Miriam Therese Winter[44]

O Christ, my Lord, again and again
I have said with Mary Magdalene,
'They have taken away my Lord
and I know not where they have laid him'.
I have been desolate and alone.
And thou hast found me again, and I know
that what has died is not thou, my Lord,
but only my idea of thee,
the image which I have made to preserve
what I have found, and to be my security.
I shall make another image, O Lord,
    better than the last.
  That too must go, and all successive images,
  until I come to the blessed vision of thyself,
  O Christ, my Lord.

George Appleton[45]

God of the empty grave,
we came to find you
where we had left you,
buried, for dead.
But you have gone ahead of us,
you have risen before us,
beyond the bounds of our feeble knowing.

Dazed by our misery and fear
we cannot interpret you:
you have gone from us,

risen into dawn,
risen into daylight.

In your great love,
wait for us
where we stumble in the garden,
till we wake
to who you are,
where you are,
risen, released in our lives.

Nicola Slee

O unfamiliar God,
we seek you in the places
you have already left,
and fail to see you
even when you stand before us.
Grant us so to recognize your strangeness
that we need not cling to our familiar grief,
but may be freed to proclaim resurrection
in the name of Christ, Amen.

Janet Morley[46]

Blessed be God for the faithfulness of Mary,
who returned to the garden on the first
Easter morning,
to seek her beloved in the tomb,
who heard her name uttered by the risen
Christ,
and found her life, her joy, her self, restored.

In her naming we hear our own names called.
In her healing we know our own wounds
healed.

In her rejoicing we enter into the freedom
and joy of the redeemed.

Make us faithful like Mary,
when faith is called forth
on the dawn of Easter morning,
Until we come at last
to share in the full glory
of Resurrection Day.

Nicola Slee[47]

EXERCISES

1 "Listen, I am the earth . . . I make everything
   grow (p.98). Much natural growth takes place
   underground, hidden and secret in the earth.
   How does this correspond to personal and spiritual growth? Does the image of the earth nurturing growth in this poem suggest possibilities
   for thinking about God?

   Go outside into your garden or any piece of
   ground where you can feel the earth beneath
   you. Take a small bowl, a trowel or old spoon
   and a notebook with you. Take off your shoes
   and socks and stand barefoot on the earth.
   Close your eyes and become aware of the earth
   supporting you, the feel of the soil under your
   feet. Open your eyes and bend down, kneeling
   on the ground. Get close to the earth and
   explore it with your hands. Dig up a small
   piece of the earth, using the trowel or spoon.
   Take some soil in your hands, feel it and smell
   it. Use the readings on pps.98-9 to meditate
   on the soil. Jot down any thoughts or insights
   in your notebook. Put the soil in your bowl and
   bring it home with you for use later on (see no.
   3 below).

2 What feelings are evoked by Frances Hodgson
   Burnett's description of Mary's discovery of the
   secret garden? What is the effect of the garden
   upon Mary? Put yourself in her place and explore

the episode through imagination, perhaps writing down Mary's thoughts in a notebook. Now do the same with Michele Roberts' portrayal of Mary Magdalene's entry into the garden on Easter morning. What similarities and differences do you note between the two episodes? Which Mary do you identify with most closely, and why?

3   "A seed is a particularly potent symbol" (p.109). Take a single seed of some variety which can be grown easily inside in a pot or outside in a window box or garden (e.g. pansy, marigold, polyanthus, etc). Take your seed into your hand. Close your eyes and feel its shape, size, hardness and weight. Become aware of its fragility as well as its potential for growth. Picture what the seed can become. What has to happen for it to grow and flower? Let the seed become a symbol of some part of your life which needs to grow. Sit quietly and ask the Spirit to direct your attention to one thing which needs to be planted and nurtured in your life. Plant your seed in the bowl of soil you took from the garden. Write down in your journal what the seed symbolizes and what you will do to make sure that part of your life flourishes. Use the poem "Seed" by Luci Shaw on p.111 as a prayer.

4   How is the coming of spring described in the poems by Robert Browning and Christina Rossetti (pp.106-7)? Write your own poem which describes how you see and experience the first signs of spring. You might also make a collection of pictures and artefacts which represent, for you, the first signs of spring. These could be

displayed during Lent in your home or church.

5   "Look long, then, here, at this budding/ of dead wood" (p.113). What does the image of dead wood suggest in this poem? How does it become a symbol of hope? Go into your garden and take from a tree or bush a single cutting of a bough which is just beginning to show the first signs of buds, but with no green. Bring the bough home and place it in a vase of water. Sit quietly and meditate on the wood. Examine its texture, its feel, its weight. Let the wood become the symbol of someone you know who is in need, pain, or whose life in some way is dead and barren. Read Ezekiel 37: 1-14 and the poem on p.113. Pray for the person and imagine them whole. Let God speak to you about their need. Is there anything God is asking you to do to further their growth and healing?

6   In the Johannine account of Mary's meeting with the Risen Christ, Mary does not immediately recognize Jesus. It is only when Jesus calls her by name that she recognizes him. Why do you think this is so? Have there been occasions in your life when you have not recognized the presence of Christ in your midst? When were they? How do you now see God acting in these times? Are there situations now in which you find it difficult to know God's presence? How might God be present, hidden and unrecognized, in these situations? Think of one situation in particular in which you find it hard to experience God's presence. Ask the Risen Christ to be present in it, and reveal himself to you. Imagine him coming into that situation and speaking your name.

What does he say to you? How do you respond?

7 "Mary was not wholly mistaken in thinking that he who addressed her was the keeper of the garden". Examine the ways in which Maria Boulding, David Middleton and Philippe de Greve (pp.108, 126-7) each develop the image of Christ as the "Gardener of thy soul". Reflect on these passages sitting quietly, perhaps outside in your garden or a nearby park. How do you imagine Christ as the Gardener? What does it mean for you to invite Christ the Gardener to work in your life? Using crayons or paint, try painting your life as a garden with Christ as the Gardener working in it. What is in your garden? What is Christ doing? What parts of your life need clearing up, weeding, pruning, planting, watering, sheltering, gathering, picking? Reflect and pray over what you have drawn or painted. Jot down what you have learnt from this exercise.

8 "Why do I kneel before your empty tomb? You are not here, for you are everywhere" (p.128). In what ways do you continue to kneel at Christ's empty tomb, searching for him when he has already left and gone on ahead of you? Think of the ways in which you limit God by searching or staying in the wrong places. Jot these down and try to think through why you act in these ways. Read and meditate on the angels' message: "He is not here. He has gone on ahead of you . . ." Use the prayers "O unfamiliar God" by Janet Morley and "God of the empty grave" by Nicola Slee on p.133 to respond to the challenge of the empty tomb.

9 Make a detailed study of the narrative of Mary's encounter with the risen Christ, using biblical commentaries to extend your own reflections and the passages in the anthology. The episode could be compared and contrasted with some of the other resurrection appearances. How does Mary's response to the Risen Christ differ from Peter's and Thomas's, for example? Which of these characters do you most identify with, and why?

10 Spring-clean your house or church, preferably with a group of friends, and decorate it with signs of spring. Afterwards, enjoy a bring-and-share meal together in the newly cleaned building and talk about how it felt to clean the place out together. How do you feel now that you have finished and can see the results of your work? Is there a need for a "spiritual spring-clean" in your own personal life or in your church/community? How could you organize such a clean-out?

3

SPRINGTIME IN THE GARDEN

Christ is Risen!

Imagine the sharp burst of sudden, certain spring, the riotous celebration of earth in the dance of the senses. The earth flings off winter's darkness, all is alive, alive. It is the season of heart's desire, of body's longing. The world rejoices, the garden is transformed.

Having discovered the secret garden, Mary Lennox is fired with a new enthusiasm and purpose. Every spare hour is spent returning to the garden to dig, weed and clear the ground. As she works with the season's turning purpose to bring the garden back to order and beauty, a powerful energy of life and vigour is let loose within the garden walls, and both child and garden find themselves responding to this life-giving energy. Mary "was becoming wider awake every day which passed at Misslethwaite. She was beginning to like to be out of doors; she no longer hated the wind, but enjoyed it. She could run faster, and longer, and she could skip up to a hundred. The bulbs in the secret garden must have been much astonished. Such nice clear spaces were made round them that they had all the breathing space they wanted, and really, if Mistress Mary had known it, they began to cheer up under the dark earth and work tremendously. The sun could get at them and warm them, and when the rain came down it could reach them at once, so they began to feel very much alive."[1] Gradually, slowly, the garden comes alive with colour, sight and sound, until the morning when Mary wakes early and knows that, at last, the spring has really come.

But Mary's secret joy in the garden cannot remain a private pleasure for long. There is a working impulse in the garden itself which seems to compel proclamation and invitation. The garden's secret is a secret which demands to be shared. Mary must learn to relinquish the prized, private delight of her discovery so that others may be admitted entry and may share the life and healing within the garden's walls.

Mary's first concession is to Dickon, Martha's brother and a kind of rustic Franciscan figure who spends most of his life wandering out on the moors. Mary has heard much about Dickon from Martha, and finally meets him one day out in the grounds, crouching under a tree, Pan-like, charming the wild creatures with his rough, wooden pipe. Mary, too, seems to fall under Dickon's spell, and before she even realizes it, she has spilled her secret of the garden. But Mary's secret is safe with Dickon, for he understands and shares her passion for the garden, and begins to work with her to clear the ground and plant new seeds. Under Dickon's watchful eye and country skills, the life in the soil is tended and cherished and the garden grows. Mary discovers, to her surprise, that the secret shared does not halve, but doubles, her pleasure. As she relinquishes her grasp on the garden and invites Dickon in, so her own joy is deepened and nurtured by Dickon's answering joy and delight in the secret. She discovers that the garden has given her a friend, and made her capable of being a friend herself.

This first move of Mary's to share her secret is only the beginning of a process which, starting from the garden and moving in ever widening circles, works outwards consistently, until all the characters in Misslethwaite Manor come to stand inside its walls and share its secret. The next stage of the process occurs when Mary shares the secret with Colin, Mr Craven's pale, ill, cross and unloved son, locked away in the heart of the rambling house's dark corridors, lying behind closed doors, sick and sorry for himself.

Mary discovers Colin one wild, wintry night. Lying in bed, listening to the wind howling around the house, she hears another sound above the wind, a "far-off faint sound of fretful crying".[2] Following the sound down the dark corridors she finally comes to a door. Pushing the door open, she finds "a big room with ancient, handsome furniture in it. There was a low fire glowing faintly on the hearth and a night-light burning by the side of a carved, four-poster bed hung with brocade, and on the bed was lying a boy, crying pitifully".[3] This is the *house's* secret of painful past buried from sight, corresponding to the grief locked and hidden in the garden. Just as Mary has burst open the locked gate of the garden and stolen its secret, opening it up to the possibility of healing, so now she bursts open the closed doors in the house and brings its hidden pain into the light of knowledge and the possibility of new life.

As the house's secret is yielded up, somehow, – gradually, unwittingly – Mary finds herself yielding up the other secret of the garden to this strange, cross, lonely boy. And just as Mary herself has been wakened to curiosity and transformation by the discovery of the garden and by her burgeoning friendship with Dickon, so, too, Colin is slowly wakened out of his crossness and sickness to life and curiosity by the sharing of the secret and the developing friendship with Mary.

The high point of Colin's transformation is reached when Mary and Dickon wheel him out into the garden itself. Colin's encounter with the garden is perhaps the most dramatic in the book, the clearest and most explicit sign of the garden's message of life and hope writ large in Colin's miraculous recovery from near death to health and strength. When Colin first comes to the garden, it is at the height of the season's glory. Everything is alive with the colour and juice and joy of the new season. Colin, in rapt amazement at what he sees and hears and feels all about him, exults in the glorious life of the garden and proclaims its secret in his glad shout, "I shall live for ever – and ever – and ever!"

Over the following weeks, Colin is brought again and again to the garden. The air and the exercise and the garden's splendour invigorate his limbs and his lust for life until first he is strong enough to stand, then to walk and finally to run. The healing and the triumph of the garden are completed when the gate is thrown wide open to welcome Ben Weatherstaff, the gardener, Dickon's mother, and Mr Craven himself to behold his strong, healthy, lively son and to come within the garden's walls.

For Mary Magdalene, too, the encounter in the garden is just a beginning. Just as she thought her life was ending in darkness and despair, she finds that it is only just starting, and she must learn to live again. She is not to stay and bask in the reunion with her Lord. She must go out and do his bidding. He is risen and she must take this news to the other disciples. The secret she has discovered in the place of burial, like Mary Lennox's, is not a secret to be guarded jealously, but a secret which demands to be shared.

The command to go, to leave her beloved whom

she has now so newly found, was perhaps experienced by Mary as a harsh and bitter blow, a rejection and denial of the intimacy she longs to prolong. The Lord she loves is sending her away. She does not want to go, she is unwilling to wrench herself from his side. Perhaps she is fearful of what she will find outside the garden, unsure of the response of his disciples to her extraordinary message. Perhaps she fears that once she leaves the garden, the whole miraculous meeting will prove to have been nothing more than a mirage, an illusion, an impossible dream. Yet, as she obeys the Lord's command – unwillingly, fearfully, even begrudgingly – she discovers the deeper miracle and truth of the resurrection, which, until now, she could not know. She finds that Christ is there, wherever she goes, the living one present with her, within her, beside her and before her, not simply manifest in the particular space and time of the garden encounter, but released in the world everywhere. As she goes out to proclaim the message of his resurrection, Christ himself has gone before her and comes after her. He makes himself present again in the company of his disciples and friends, and teaches them that henceforth he will be with them always in the power and presence of the Spirit. He is no longer to be known within the confines of his own physical body, but will manifest himself in the body of his believers, in the bodies of those who love him and receive him, in the lovely body of the earth itself. Earth, air, sky, sun, moon, water, fire and all that is within the world henceforth have become God's body and proclaim God's glory.

And Mary, too, must learn to know him in this bigger, wider, deeper, freer way. She who had defined herself wholly in terms of her relationship to him, her saviour, healer, lover, lord and friend, is now to let him go, and find herself and her God in a new freedom and openness of being. Released from the bonds of a clinging, cloying love and dependency upon Jesus, she is to become her own true self in freedom and share that self freely and generously with other selves – friends, lovers, sisters, brothers. She who had first met and known God in the beloved body of Jesus is now to meet and know the same divine presence in her own beloved woman's body, in the body of other believers, in the body of all God's creatures, in the body of the world. Paradoxically, only by thus stepping out into separation and freedom, by letting her Christ go freely, will she find him and know him in all the abundance of wholeness, joy and fulness which he promises. Unfettered by time and space, unlimited by the physical body which Mary had loved and has learned to let go, the Lord will be with them and among them in radically new and unexpected ways.

For the two Marys, this final turning outwards to share, proclaim and celebrate the garden secret with others is the continuing impulse and ongoing momentum of the Easter season. It is the celebration of the world's springtime. Daring to risk the ridicule, spoiling and dispossession of their most precious secret in the garden, they have turned outwards and offered this gift to others. And in doing so, they have discovered the enduring miracle of resurrection – that where death and loss are risked, there life can take root and something unheard of will grow and flower. In sharing their own healed and restored selves with others, in opening the garden gate and

welcoming others in, they have found that their
own joy and renewal is multiplied a hundredfold
in the healing and restoration granted to others
who enter into their joyful proclamation and accept
it for themselves. In telling their own good news,
the two Marys allow the Eastering Spirit to work
the same good news of resurrection in others. Their
own healed and restored lives become the place of
meeting and healing for others.

This is the dynamic momentum of Easter faith.
The secret discovery of the individual self is released
and risked into the wider community and its joy is
taken up and multiplied in the response of others
to the signs of healing and renewal they have
seen in the proclaimers' lives. Renewed and healed
themselves, these others take the message up and
proclaim it to others again. The Easter process which
began with the solitary encounter – God and God's
future entrusted to the passionate love of a jealous
yet faithful woman – ripples outwards into the
whole of human history. Enfleshed and incarnated
again in the emboldened lives of those who believe
the woman's word, the Easter Christ is set free in
the world.

Nor does the Easter miracle end with the transformation of human lives. In the Easter hope is
proclaimed a hope for the entire created order. Let
loose in the world, the risen Christ is become Lord
of the universe, manifest in the whole cosmos, and
Christians see the signs of this in the workings of
the natural world. As the seasons turn in their
cycle of death and regeneration, and springtime
erupts in the passion of nature reborn, the Easter
Christ is to be seen and heard, tasted and touched,
loved and longed for, wherever the eye turns. In the

abundance of colour, sound, growth and fragrance, Christ is celebrated and proclaimed as risen and embodied in the world. This is the lesson the Marys learn. The garden walls where they first found and knew him widen to include the whole world in the springtime of the year. And, though the seasons will turn and death will come again, though suffering and anguish continue in the world, though Christ must be nailed on the cross again in the darkness of the world's turning, yet this eruption of life and wholeness at Easter is the guarantee and first-fruits of that wholeness and justice which all the world longs for, and which God has promised to deliver in the end.

On that first morning when the sky was blue again, Mary wakened very early. The sun was pouring in slanting rays through the blinds and there was something so joyous in the sight of it that she jumped out of bed and ran to the window. She drew up the blinds and opened the window itself, and a great waft of fresh, scented air blew in upon her. The moor was blue and the whole world looked as if something Magic had happened to it. There were tender little fluting sounds here and there and everywhere, as if scores of birds were beginning to tune up for a concert. Mary put her hand out of the window and held it in the sun.

"It's warm – warm!" she said. "It will make the green points push up and up and up, and it will make the bulbs and roots work and struggle with all their might under the earth."

She kneeled down and leaned out of the window as far as she could, breathing big breaths and sniffing the air until she laughed . . .

"It must be very early," she said. "The little clouds are all pink and I've never seen the sky look like this. No one is up. I don't even hear the stable-boys."

A sudden thought made her scramble to her feet. "I can't wait! I am going to see the garden!"

She had learnt to dress herself by this time, and she put on her clothes in five minutes. She knew a small side door which she could unbolt herself, and she flew downstairs in her stocking feet and put on her shoes in the hall. She unchained and unbolted and unlocked, and when the door was open she sprang across the step with one bound, and there she was standing on the grass, which seemed to have turned green, and with the sun pouring down on her and warm, sweet wafts about her and the fluting and twittering and singing coming from every bush and tree. She clasped her hands for pure joy and looked up in the sky, and it was so blue and pink and pearly and white and flooded with springtime light that she felt as if she must flute and sing aloud herself, and knew that thrushes and robins and sky-larks could not possibly help it. She ran around the shrubs and paths towards the secret garden.

"It is all different already," she said. "The grass is greener and things are sticking up everywhere and things are uncurling and green buds of leaves are showing. This afternoon I am sure Dickon will come."

The long warm rain had done strange things to the herbaceous beds which bordered the walk by the lower wall. There were things sprouting and pushing out from the roots of clumps of plants and there were actually here and there glimpses of royal purple and yellow unfurling among the the stems of crocuses. Six months before Mistress Mary would not have seen how the world was waking up, but now she missed nothing.

. . . When she got fairly into the garden she saw . . . the stooping body and rust-red head of Dickon, who was kneeling on the grass working hard.

Mary flew across the grass to him.

"Oh, Dickon! Dickon!" she cried out. "How could you get here so early! How could you!

The sun has only just got up!"

He got up himself, laughing and glowing, and tousled; his eyes like a bit of the sky.

"Eh!" he said. "I was up long before him. How could I have stayed abed! Th' world's all fair begun again this mornin', it has. An' it's workin' an' hummin' an' scratchin' an' pipin' an' nest-buildin' an' breathin' out scents, till you've got to be out on it 'stead o' lyin' on your back. When th' sun did jump up, th' moor went mad for joy, an' I was in the midst of th' heather, an' I ran like mad myself, shoutin' an' singin'. An' I come straight here. I couldn't have stayed away. Why, th' garden was lyin' here waitin'!"

Mary put her hands on her chest, panting, as if she had been running herself.

"Oh, Dickon! Dickon!" she said. 'I'm so happy I can scarcely breathe!"

They ran from one part of the garden to another and found so many wonders that they were obliged to remind themselves that they must whisper or speak low. He showed her swelling leaf-buds on rose branches which had seemed dead. He showed her ten thousand new green points pushing through the mould. They put their eager young noses close to the earth and sniffed its warmed springtime breathing; they dug and pulled and laughed low with rapture until Mistress Mary's hair was as tumbled as Dickon's and her cheeks were almost as poppy red as his.

There was every joy on earth in the secret garden that morning.

Frances Hodgson Burnett[4]

Where wind sings green on lamb-nibbled paths
where air is brushed by the seep of sharp wings
and the sun-heaped flowers stare
a child-stare
till I could scoop them up
to lull in my arms,
that note –
is it light, water or bird?
This breath I feel on my brow
is it fragrance of pear-blossom?

I am drunk and drink for evermore
this adoration.
No song before
was ever poured in this pure modulation.
I do not know
if I am looking on
sun
earth or flower
for all the world today
rings mad
with exultation.

Sister Mary Agnes[5]

And joy is everywhere; it is in the earth's
green covering of grass; in the blue serenity of
the sky; in the reckless exuberance of spring;
in the severe abstinence of grey winter; in the
living flesh that animates our bodily frame; in
the perfect poise of the human figure, noble
and upright; in living; in the exercise of all
our powers; in the acquisition of knowledge;
in fighting evils; in dying for gains we never
can share. Joy is there everywhere; it is super-
fluous, unnecessary; nay, it very often contra-

dicts the most peremptory behests of necessity. It exists to show that the bonds of law can only be explained by love; they are like body and soul. Joy is the realization of the truth of oneness, the oneness of our soul with the world and of the world-soul with the supreme lover.

Rabindranath Tagore[6]

The same stream of life that runs through my veins night and day runs through the world and dances in rhythmic measures.

It is the same life that shoots in joy through the dust of the earth in the numberless blades of grass and breaks into tumultuous waves of leaves and flowers.

It is the same life that is rocked in the ocean-cradle of birth and death, in ebb and in flow.

I feel my limbs are made glorious by the touch of this world of life. And my pride is from the lifethrob of ages dancing in my blood this moment.

Rabindranath Tagore[7]

All that is sweet, delightful, and amiable in this world, in the serenity of the air, the fineness of seasons, the joy of light, the melody of sounds, the beauty of colours, the fragrancy of smells, the splendour of precious stones, is nothing else but Heaven breaking through the veil of this world, manifesting itself in such a degree and darting forth in such variety so much of its own nature.

William Law[8]

The universe is the overflowing of God's Joy, the calling into existence of further otherness to which in Joy God gives himself so that in Joy it may correspondingly give itself to him . . .

As God's Joy grows within us it enables us to perceive his Joy in the world around us. And just as within ourselves God's Joy is often hidden like the mustard seed in the earth, so, too, around us it will often be hidden under this or another disguise . . . In all the Joy of God lies waiting with infinite patience for its appointed time, working continually on every kind of recalcitrant raw material until it can deliver as golden what formerly was brazen. And . . . we can perceive God's Joy thus secretly at work in those around us because that same Joy is also at work within us.

H. A. Williams[9]

That night Colin slept without once awakening, and when he opened his eyes in the morning he lay still and smiled without knowing it – smiled because he felt so curiously comfortable. It was actually nice to be awake, and he turned over and stretched his limbs luxuriously . . . He had not been awake more than ten minutes when he heard feet running along the corridor and Mary was at the door. The next minute she was in the room and had run across to his bed, bringing with her a waft of fresh air full of the scent of the morning.

"You've been out! You've been out! There's that nice smell of leaves!" he cried.

She had been running and her hair was loose
and blown, and she was bright with the air and
pink-cheeked . . .

"It's so beautiful!" she said, a little breathless with her speed. "You never saw anything
so beautiful! It has *come*! I thought it had
come that other morning, but it was only coming. It is here now! It has come, the Spring!"
. . .

"Has it?" cried Colin, and though he really
knew nothing about it, he felt his heart beat.
He actually sat up in bed.

"Open the window!" he added, laughing half
with joyful excitement and half at his own
fancy. "Perhaps we may hear golden trum-
pets!"

And though he laughed, Mary was at the
window in a moment and in a moment more
it was opened wide and freshness and softness and scents and birds' songs were pouring
through.

"That's fresh air," she said. "Lie on your back
and draw in long breaths of it. That's what
Dickon does when he's lying on the moor. He
says he feels it in his veins and it makes him
strong and he feels as if he could live for ever
and ever. Breathe it and breathe it."

She was only repeating what Dickon had
told her, but she caught Colin's fancy.

" 'For ever and ever!' Does it make him feel
like that?" he said, and he did as she told him,
drawing in long deep breaths over and over
again, until he felt that something quite new
and delightful was happening to him.

Mary was at his bedside again.

"Things are crowding up out of the earth," she ran on in a hurry. "And there are flowers uncurling and buds on everything and the green veil has covered nearly all the grey and the birds are in such a hurry about their nests for fear they may be too late, that some of them are even fighting for places in the secret garden. And the rosebushes look as wick as wick can be, and there are primroses in the lanes and woods, and the seeds we planted are up . . ."

Frances Hodgson Burnett[10]

Unfold, unfold! take in his light,
Who makes thy cares more short than night.
The joys, which with his day-star rise,
He deals to all, but drowsy eyes:
And what the men of this world miss,
Some drops and dews of future bliss.

Hark, how his winds have chang'd their note,
And with warm whispers call thee out.
The frosts are past, the storms are gone:
And backward life at last comes on.
The lofty groves in express joys
Reply unto the turtle's voice,
And here in dust and dirt, O here
The lilies of his love appear!

Henry Vaughan[11]

Arise, my love, my fair one,
  and come away;
for lo, the winter is past,
  the rain is over and gone.

The flowers appear on the earth,
   the time of singing has come,
and the voice of the turtledove
   is heard in our land.
The fig tree puts forth its figs,
    and the vines are in blossom;
   they give forth fragrance.
Arise, my love, my fair one,
   and come away.

                Song of Songs 2: 10-13

I got me flowers to straw thy way;
I got me boughs off many a tree:
But thou wast up by break of day,
And brought'st thy sweets along with thee.

The Sunne arising in the East,
Though he give light, and th' East perfume;
If they should offer to contest
With thy arising, they presume.

Can there be any day but this,
Though many sunnes to shine endeavour?
We count three hundred, but we misse:
There is but one and that one ever.

               George Herbert[12]

If ever I saw blessing in the air
I see it now in this still early day
Where lemon-green the vaporous morning
   drips
Wet sunlight on the powder of my eye.

Blown bubble-film of blue, the sky wraps round
Weeds of warm light whose every root and rod
Splutters with soapy green, and all the world
Sweats with the bead of summer in its bud.

If ever I heard blessing it is there
Where birds in trees that shoals and shadows are
Splash with their hidden wings and drops of sound
Break on my ears their crests of throbbing air.

Pure in the haze the emerald sun dilates
The lips of sparrows milk the mossy stones,
While white as water by the lake a girl
Swims her green hand among the gathered swans.

Now, as the almond burns its smoking wick,
Dropping small flames to light the candled grass;
Now, as my low blood scales its second chance,
If ever world were blessed, now it is.

Laurie Lee[13]

This is the day which the Lord has made;
   let us rejoice and be glad in it.

Sing, O heavens, for the Lord has done it;
   shout, O depths of the earth;
break forth into singing, O mountains,
   O forest, and every tree in it!
For the Lord has redeemed Jacob,
   and will be glorified in Israel.

Sing for joy, O heavens, and exult, O earth;
   break forth, O mountains, into singing!
For the Lord has comforted his people,
   and will have compassion on his afflicted.

This is the day which the Lord has made;
   let us rejoice and be glad in it.

Psalm 118:24; Isaiah 44:23, 49:13; Psalm 118:24

i thank You God for most this amazing
day: for the leaping greenly spirits of trees
and a blue true dream of sky; and for everything
which is natural which is infinite which is yes

(i who have died am alive again today,
and this is the sun's birthday; this is the birth
day of life and of love and wings: and of the
  gay
great happening illimitably earth)

how should tasting touching hearing seeing
breathing any – lifted from the no
of all nothing – human merely being
doubt unimaginable You?

(now the ears of my ears awake and
now the eyes of my eyes are opened)

                    e.e. cummings[14]

All you works of God, bless your creator;
praise her and glorify her for ever.

Let the wide earth bless the creator;
let the arching heavens bless the creator;
let the whole body of God bless the creator;
praise her and glorify her for ever.

You returning daylight, bless your creator;
twilight and shadows, bless your creator;
embracing darkness, bless your creator;
praise her and glorify her for ever.

Mountains of God, massive and ancient rocks,
  bless your creator;
valleys and pastures, moorland and rivers,
  bless your creator;
ocean depths and lonely abyss,
    bless your creator;
    praise her and glorify her for ever.

  Storm and mighty wind, bless your creator;
  bitter cold and scorching sun, bless your
    creator;
  mist and cloud and tender rain, bless your
    creator;
  praise her and glorify her for ever.

Seed and sapling, tree and vivid flower, bless
    your creator;
greenness and flourishing, withering and
    bareness, bless your creator;
harvest and springtime and deadness of
    the year, bless your creator;
  praise her and glorify her for ever.

You creatures of God, bless your creator;
swift and cunning, violent and graceful, bless
    your creator;
all who creep and soar and dance across the
    earth, bless your creator;
praise her and glorify her for ever.

You newborn babies, bless your creator;
young and old, mature and ageing, bless your
    creator;
all you dying, bless your creator;
praise her and glorify her for ever.

In pain and desolation, let us bless our creator;

in the place of delight, let us bless our creator;
in time of waiting, let us bless our creator;
praise her and glorify her for ever.

Let all who live and grow and breathe bless
    our creator;
praise her and glorify her for ever.
                              Janet Morley[15]

The passion of God broke through in Christ,
and in him it is breaking through once more.
It is breaking through in a new way, but we are
enabled to perceive its newness because what
we are seeing causes constant little shocks of
recognition. It has not "happened before" yet it
is piercingly familiar, as each spring is unique,
yet recognized in its uniqueness as the breakthrough of an eternal newness, deeply familiar
yet never to be held, always to be freshly discovered.

Like spring, this breakthrough of newness
is violent. We are sentimental about spring
. . . But spring is not gentle or cosy. It is an
eruption of life so strong it can push bricks
apart and make houses fall down. It thrusts
through . . . layers of rotted past. The diamond
brilliance of the cuckoo's note is the result of
many fledglings shouldered out of the nest to
their deaths, as all new life thrusts aside whatever impedes it. Even in the sheer perfection of
each growing thing there is an integrity which
is painful in its accuracy. The scent of lilacs in
the dawn cuts through fuzziness of disordered
desire, the etched whiteness of lily of the val-
ley against dark leaves sears the imagination.

These are not soft things; they have a tenderness ascetically fined down to an essential longing. This is the violence of absolute love, which takes the Kingdom of Heaven by storm in a silence of total concentration on the one thing necessary.

Rosemary Haughton[16]

In itself, passion is an irrational power with both destructive and creative potential, requiring intention to direct its creative human possibilities. It can destroy us from within. But harnessed and so integrated into the human personality, its dynamic power can transform and give meaning to human life and death. When, therefore, God is a person's true centre and whole intention, passion releases from the pure intent of the will a strength and dynamic power of energy that gains in momentum from its unified direction. Then the person is both liberated from all that is not ordered to God, and somehow carried, in the powerful flow of passionate love, towards God. Passion, then, is a yearning, a reaching out, with every fibre of the body-person to the fullness of life and meaning in God. It is an intense psycho-physical thrust of the whole person, that focuses all our sensibilities and fuses all our faculties into one unifying process directed towards union with God.

Pamela Hayes[17]

Jesus said to Mary, "Do not hold me, for I have not yet ascended to the Father; but go to my brethren and say to them, I am ascending

to my Father and your Father, to my God and
your God." Mary Magdalene went and said to
the disciples, "I have seen the Lord"; and she
told them that he had said these things to her.

John 20: 17-18

You shall be my witnesses through all the earth,
telling of all you have heard and received,
for I arose and am with you, and you have
  believed.

  Women at the tomb,
  weeping for the dead.
  He is not here,
  he has risen as he said.
  They ran to tell those who were in authority.
  The men dismissed the news as idle fantasy.

You shall be my witnesses through all the earth,
telling of all you have heard and received,
for I arose and am with you, and you have
  believed.

  Magdalene at the tomb:
  Whom do you seek?
  Her eyes were opened
  when she heard him speak.
  His love for every woman shone upon his face.
  The hopes of every age were held in their
    embrace.

You shall be my witnesses through all the earth,
telling of all you have heard and received,
for I arose and am with you, and you have
  believed.

Women, leave your tombs.
Roll the stones aside.
Do not despair,
though so many dreams have died.
Do not be fearful of the vision that you see.
Believe in miracles again. Believe in me.

You shall be my witnesses through all the earth,
telling of all you have heard and received,
for I arose and am with you, and you have
    believed.

Miriam Therese Winter[18]

Sisters and Brothers – Arise.
Arise and lift your hearts
Arise and lift your eyes
Arise and lift your voices.

The living God,
The living, moving Spirit of God
has called us together –
in witness
in celebration
in struggle.

Reach out toward each other.
Our God reaches out toward us!
Let us worship God!

Elizabeth Rice[19]

It suddenly strikes me
with overwhelming force:

It was women
who were the first to spread the message of

Easter –
the unheard of!

It was women
who rushed to the disciples,
who, breathless and bewildered,
passed on the greatest message of all:

He is alive!

Think if women had kept silence
in the churches!

Marta Wilhelmsson[20]

My heart is bubbling over with joy;
with God it is good to be woman.
From now on let all peoples proclaim:
it is a wonderful gift to be.
The one in whom power truly rests
has lifted us up to praise;
God's goodness shall fall like a shower
on the trusting of every age.
The disregarded have been raised up:
the pompous and powerful shall fall.
God has feasted the empty-bellied,
and the rich have discovered their void.
God has made good the word
given at the dawn of time.

Phoebe Willetts[21]

We told our stories –
That's all.
We sat and listened to
Each other
And heard the journeys

Of each soul.
We sat in silence
Entering each one's pain and
Sharing each one's joy.
We heard love's longing
And the lonely reachings-out
For love and affirmation.
We heard of dreams
Shattered.
And visions fled.
Of hopes and laughter
Turned stale and dark.
We felt the pain of
Isolation and
The bitterness
Of death.

But in each brave and
Lonely story
God's gentle life
Broke through
And we heard music in
The darkness
And smelt flowers in
The void.

We felt the budding
Of creation
In the searchings of
Each soul
And discerned the beauty
Of God's hand in
Each muddy, twisted path.

And His voice sang
In each story

His life sprang from
Each death.
Our sharing became
One story
Of a simple lonely search
For life and hope and
Oneness
In a world which sobs
For love.
And we knew that in
Our sharing
God's voice with
Mighty breath
Was saying
Love each other and
Take each other's hand.

For you are one
Though many
And in each of you
I live.
So listen to my story
And share my pain
And death.

Oh, listen to my story
And rise and live
With me.

Edwina Gateley[22]

A little later the nurse made Colin ready . . .
The strongest footman in the house carried
Colin downstairs and put him in his wheeled-
chair, near which Dickon waited outside . . .

Dickon began to push the wheeled-chair
slowly and steadily. Mistress Mary walked

beside it and Colin leaned back and lifted his face to the sky. The arch of it looked very high and the small snowy clouds seemed like white birds floating on outspread wings below its crystal blueness. The wind swept in soft big breaths down from the moor and was strange with a wild clear-scented sweetness. Colin kept lifting his thin chest to draw it in, and his big eyes looked as if it were they which were listening – listening, instead of his ears.

"There are so many sounds of singing and humming and calling out," he said. "What is that scent the puffs of wind bring?"

"It's gorse on th' moor that's openin' out," answered Dickon . . .

Not a human creature was to be caught sight of in the paths they took . . . They wound in and out among the shrubbery and out and round the fountain beds, following their carefully planned route for the mere mysterious pleasure of it. But when at last they turned into the Long Walk by the ivied walls, the excited sense of an approaching thrill made them, for some curious reason they could not have explained, begin to speak in whispers.

"This is it," breathed Mary. "This is where I used to walk up and down and wonder and wonder."

"Is it?" cried Colin, and his eyes began to search the ivy with eager curiousness. "But I can see nothing," he whispered. "There is no door."

"That's what I thought," said Mary.

Then there was a lovely, breathless silence and the chair wheeled on . . . A few yards more and Mary whispered again.

"This is where the robin flew over the wall," she said.

"Is it?" cried Colin. "Oh! I wish he'd come again!"

"And that," said Mary with solemn delight, pointing under a big lilac bush, "is where he perched on the little heap of earth and showed me the key."

Then Colin sat up.

"Where? Where? There?" he cried, and his eyes were as big as the wolf's in Red Riding Hood . . . Dickon stood still and the wheeled-chair stopped.

"And this," said Mary, stepping onto the bed close to the ivy, "is where I went to talk to him when he chirped at me from the top of the wall. And this is the ivy the wind blew back," and she took hold of the hanging green curtain.

"Oh! is it – " gasped Colin.

"And here is the handle, and here is the door. Dickon, push him in – push him in quickly!"

And Dickon did it with one strong, steady, splendid push.

But Colin had actually dropped back against his cushions, even though he gasped with delight, and he had covered his eyes with his hands and held them there, shutting out everything until they were inside and the chair stopped as if by magic and the door was closed. Not till then did he take them away and look round and round and round as Dickon and Mary had done. And over walls and earth and trees and swinging sprays and tendrils the fair green veil of tender little leaves had crept, and in the grass under the trees and the grey urns in the alcoves and here and there everywhere, were touches or splashes of gold and purple and white and the trees were showing pink and snow above his head, and there were fluttering of wings and faint sweet pipes and humming and scents and scents. And the sun fell warm upon his face like a hand with a lovely touch. And in wonder Mary and Dickon stood and stared at him. He looked so strange and different because a pink glow of colour had actually crept all over him – ivory face and neck and hands and all.

"I shall get well! I shall get well!" he cried out. "Mary! Dickon! I shall get well! And I shall live for ever and ever and ever!"

Frances Hodgson Burnett[23]

Spring has come for [us] today!
Christ has burst his prison,
and from three days' sleep in death
like the sun has risen.
All the winter of our sins,
long and dark, is dying:
welcome now the light of Christ,
life and joy supplying!

J. M. Neale[24]

Now the green blade riseth from the buried grain,
wheat that in the dark earth many days has lain;
Love lives again, that with the dead has been:
  Love is come again,
  like wheat that springeth green.

In the grave they laid him, Love whom men
  had slain,
thinking that never he would wake again,
laid in the earth like grain that sleeps unseen:
  Love is come again,
  like wheat that springeth green.

Forth he came at Easter, like the risen grain,
he that for three days in the grave had lain,
quick from the dead my risen Lord is seen:
  Love is come again,
  like wheat that springeth green.

                     J.M.C. Crum[25]

      Have you seen the
      wonder year by year
      earth's in-sowing
      secretly inwrought
      seed flower fruit and
      seed again in-falls

      have you seen the
      wonder day by day
      Christ in-sowing Christ
      through wheat and vine
      our fruit-bearing Christ
      to glorify the source.
        A sister of St Mary's Abbey[26]

Corn King
  spring!
leap, leap. Lord of light,
dance, dance, dear delight.

Grain buried deep
today, tomorrow, sleep

then
lightward
larkward
skyward
Godward
  leap
bright to death

Broken corn King harvested,
thrashed, ground, milled for bread
  at daylight leap
from your dark sleep.

Harvester, begin
the dance, the dear delight.
Yielded sheaves, golden bright,
  a garnered horde
welcome their harvest lord
while corn-fat valleys shout and sing
  honouring
the harvest king,
  feasting
the harvest home
with broken bread and one cry: *Come!*
                    Jenny Robertson[27]

Unless a grain of wheat falls into the earth
and dies, it remains alone; but if it dies, it
bears much fruit.

What you sow does not come to life unless it
dies. And what you sow is not the body which
is to be, but a bare kernel, perhaps of wheat or
of some other grain. But God gives it a body as
he has chosen, and to each kind of seed its own
body . . .

What is sown is perishable, what is raised is imperishable. It is sown in dishonour, it is raised in glory. It is sown in weakness, it is raised in power . . .
When the perishable puts on the imperishable, and the mortal puts on immortality, then shall come to pass the saying that is written:

> *"Death is swallowed up in victory."*
> *"O death, where is thy victory?*
> *O death, where is thy sting?"*

Thanks be to God, who gives us the victory through our Lord Jesus Christ.
John 12: 24; I Corinthians 15: 36-38,
42-43, 54-55, 57

The dying leaves of a hundred million autumns have built up the humus from which our crops spring . . . A hard, polished acorn falls to the ground and cracks open, but it sends one shoot down and another up, and later there is a tree. Life springs and grows where the bearers of life do not clutch it to themselves, but hear the call to let it go in the interests of fuller life and action. The caterpillar consents to the cocoon, sensing its destiny.

Maria Boulding[28]

God's glory clothes creation, and the Eastering Spirit is already transfiguring our mortality, though our angle of vision seldom allows us to see it . . .

In spite of the fearful precariousness of creation, God believes in the power of life which he has planted in us amid so much risk. The grain of wheat risks absolute loss and seems indeed to die in the dark, cold earth, but it is charged with the energy of hidden new life, and its time of glory will come. So the kingdom of God is being built, secretly and with the everlasting patience of love.

Maria Boulding[29]

God's Word is in all creation,
   visible and invisible.
The Word
is living,
being,
spirit,
all verdant greening,
all creativity.
All creation
is awakened,
called,
by the resounding melody,
God's invocation of the Word.
This Word manifests in every creature.

I am the one whose praise
echoes on high.
I adorn all the earth.
I am the breeze
that nurtures all things
green.
I encourage blossoms to flourish with ripening
    fruits.
I am led by the spirit to feed

the purest streams.
　I am the rain
　coming from the dew
　that causes the grasses to laugh
　with the joy of life.
　Invisible life that sustains all,
　I awaken to life everything
　in every waft of air.
　The air is life,
　greening and blossoming.
　The waters flow with life.
　The sun is lit with life.
　The moon, when waning, is again
　　rekindled by the sun,
　　　waxing with life once more.
　The stars shine,
　radiating with life-light.
　All creation is gifted with the
　ecstasy of God's light.
　There is
　no creation
　that does not have a radiance
　　be it greenness or seed,
　　　blossom or beauty.
　It could not be creation without it.
　　　　　　Hildegard of Bingen[30]

Christhasrisen,ourtruesuninthedarknessofthenight.
And the bees fly here and there, rejoicing in
　their work,
Noisily collecting honey from the flowers,
　　white and red.
Birds of many kinds make soft the air with
　　singing,

And nightly now the nightingale pours out her
   lovely notes.
Now churches too are filled with the sound
   of chanting,
As the people sing their Alleluias, Alleluias
   hundredfold.

Sedulius Scotus[31]

No human eye was by
To witness Christ arise,
But I, this morning heard
The Resurrection of the Word.

It sprang through night, opaque,
A note so pure and clear,
I felt my spirit wake –
It flooded everywhere.

I know that it has been;
There is a vision new.
I see the universe
Divinely bathed in dew.

Sister Mary Agnes[32]

Easter, Christ Risen, the Risen Lord, this, to the
old faith, is still the first day in the year. The
Easter festivities are the most joyful, the Easter
processions the finest, the Easter ceremonies
the most splendid. In Sicily the women take
into church the saucers of growing corn, the
green blades rising tender and slim like green
light, in little pools, filling round the altar. It
is Adonis. It is the re-born year. It is Christ
Risen. It is the Risen Lord. And in the warm

south still a great joy floods the hearts of the people on Easter Sunday. They feel it, they feel it everywhere. The Lord is risen. The Lord of the rising wheat and the plum blossoms is warm and kind upon the earth again, after having been done to death by the evil and the jealous ones . . .

This is the image of the young: the Risen Lord. The teaching is over, the crucifixion is over, the sacrifice is made, the salvation is accomplished. Now comes the true life, [humanity] living [our] full life on earth, as flowers live their full life, without rhyme or reason except the magnificence of coming forth into fullness.

D.H. Lawrence[33]

The Resurrection is now! In the midst of life we are in death, day by day we come to all sorts of ends, we meet defeat and the dying of our hopes, and the Father meets us there too. In the midst of life we are in the Resurrection. The Resurrection is now, as well as then; it is here, as well as there . . . We can have confidence that he will be with us at the end of all ends, because we can experience him in the midst of the endless endingness that characterizes our life now. But the process is always the same: we meet the Father only when we have gone through the dying. The Resurrection is never an evasion of death, it is consequent upon death, it only comes when we have plumbed the depths . . . At the very moment of hopelessness, when we confront, possibly for the first time, what we really are, that very moment is the Resurrection now! . . .

The Resurrection is not just about the reconstitution of the broken body of Christ into an eternal and ineffaceable glory. It is a pledge to us, a sign that God is at work now, restoring his damaged creation to its original pattern. And it is costly work, bloody work, because evil is real and its tentacles range through time. Here, too, we must accept the reality of death, the reality of our situation; we must, somehow, say "yes" to the dying of the light . . .

And it is the testimony of many, that even here the Resurrection is now, though it creeps upon us unawares . . . Come it does, as a lifting and lessening of a burden, a quiet sense of release, a sense that the night is, at last, over and gone. If we wait for it, it will come. It is the experience of the Resurrection now. For the Christian it comes supremely in that strange, broken image of the young Christ setting his face towards Calvary to die there. But another image replaces that one, without completely removing it, so that we see both at once. We continue to see that endless going up to Calvary, and that suffering and that dying. Then there is that hush before dawn in the garden where they laid him. No movement. Only the strange and wistful twilight of yesterday's grave. And then a sudden and terrible glory rises from that ancient sorrow. Suffering itself is transfigured and that dying becomes the Resurrection.

Richard Holloway[34]

The wilderness and the dry land shall be glad,
    the desert shall rejoice and blossom;
like the crocus it shall blossom abundantly,
    and rejoice with joy and singing.
The glory of Lebanon shall be given to it,
    the majesty of Carmel and Sharon.
They shall see the glory of the Lord,
    the majesty of our God.

Strengthen the weak hands,
    and make firm the feeble knees.
Say to those who are of a fearful heart,
    "Be strong, fear not!
Behold, your God will come with vengeance,
    with the recompense of God.
He will come and save you."

Then the eyes of the blind shall be opened,
    and the ears of the deaf unstopped;
then shall the lame man leap like a hart,
    and the tongue of the dumb sing for joy.
For waters shall break forth in the wilderness,
    and streams in the desert;
the burning sand shall become a pool,
    and the thirsty ground springs of water;
the haunt of jackals shall become a swamp,
    the grass shall become reeds and rushes.

And the ransomed of the Lord shall return,
    and come to Zion with singing;
everlasting joy shall be upon their heads;
    they shall obtain joy and gladness,

and sorrow and sighing shall flee away.
                              Isaiah 35: 1-7, 9-10

And then all that has divided us will merge
And then compassion will be wedded to power
And then softness will come to a world that
    is harsh and unkind
And then both men and women will be gentle
    And then both women and men will be strong
And then no person will be subject to another's
    will
And then all will be rich and free and var-
    ied
And then the greed of some will give way to
    the needs of many
And then all will share equally in the Earth's
    abundance
And then all will care for the sick and
    the
    weak and the old
And then all will nourish the young
And then all will cherish life's creatures.
And then all will live in harmony with each
    other and the Earth
And then everywhere will be called Eden
    once again.
                              Judy Chicago[35]

Things beyond our seeing, things beyond our
    hearing,
things beyond our imagining,
all prepared by God for those who love him –
these it is that God has revealed to us through
    the Spirit.

No longer need we teach one another to know
  the Lord;
all of us shall know him, high and low alike.
Now at last God has his dwelling among men
   [and women]
They shall be his people and god himself will
   be with them.
He will wipe away every tear from their eyes;
there shall be an end to death, and to mourning
  and crying and pain;
For the old order has passed away . . .
Behold! I am making all things new!
     I Corinthians 2: 9-10; Jeremiah 31:34;
                Revelation 21:4-5

  It's a long way off but inside it
  There are quite different things going on:
  Festivals at which the poor man
  Is king and the consumptive is
  Healed; mirrors in which the blind look
  At themselves and love looks at them
  Back; and industry is for mending
  The bent bones and the minds fractured
  By life. It's a long way off, but to get
  There takes no time and admission
  Is free, if you will purge yourself
  Of desire, and present yourself with
  Your need only and the simple offering
  Of your faith, green as a leaf.
                R.S. Thomas[36]

PRAYERS

God of all our growing,
burst our tight buds open
in the ripe spring season
  of our transformation.
Nurture the resurrection life in us,
in the blazing colour of the garden,
in the dazzling delight of sight and sound,
  the glorious celebration of the world's
      redemption.
    Send your Spirit where the glad season rejoices
    and fulfil in us the promise of spring.

Nicola Slee

Lord of all life and power,
who through the mighty resurrection of your
Son
overcame the old order of sin and death
to make all things new in him:
grant that we, being dead to sin
and alive to you in Jesus Christ,
may reign with him in glory;
to whom with you and the Holy Spirit
be praise and honour, glory and might,
now and in all eternity.

Alternative Service Book 1980[37]

Lord our God, the universe celebrates you and
all creatures proclaim your power. Receive this

morning the songs we raise and renew the gifts
of your grace, through Jesus Christ, your Son,
our Lord.

Taizé collect[38]

Glorious Lord, I give you greeting!
Let the church and the chancel praise you,
Let the chancel and the church praise you,
Let the plain and the hillside praise you,
Let the world's three well-springs praise you,
Two above wind and one above land,
Let the dark and the daylight praise you . . .
Let the life everlasting praise you,
Let the birds and honeybees praise you,
Let the shorn stems and the shoots praise you
. . .
Let the male and the female praise you,
Let the seven days and the stars praise you,
Let the air and the ether praise you,
Let the books and the letters praise you,
Let the fish in the swift streams praise you,
Let the thought and the action praise you,
Let the sand-grains and the earth-clods
    praise you,
Let all the good that's performed praise you.
And I shall praise you, Lord of glory:
Glorious Lord, I give you greeting.

Traditional Celtic[39]

Thou whose brow is of snow, whose eyes are
of fire, whose feet are more dazzling than gold
poured from the furnace; Thou whose hands
hold captive the stars, Thou the first and the
last, the living, the dead and risen again; Thou

who dost gather up in Thy superabundant oneness every delight, every taste, every energy,
every phase of existence, to Thee my being cries
out with a longing as vast as the universe, for
Thou indeed art my Lord and my God.

Teilhard de Chardin[40]

Ah, Lord our God, if Thou art so lovely in
Thy creatures, how exceedingly beautiful and
ravishing Thou must be in Thyself!

Henry Suso[41]

> You are lovely, God!
>   From the pitch of the
> sky they must tell You:
>   the angels, squads of
> angels, must tell You,
>   sun, moon, stars of the
> morning must tell You,
>   the rain overhead
> in store must tell You,
>   You are lovely, God!
> All loveliness comes
>   from Your decision!
> You made it to stay
>   where You ordered it,
> never to pass away!
>   From the pitch of the
> deeps they must tell You,
>   sea monsters and all!
> The fire here, the smoke,
>   the hail, the snow, the wind
> storming to obey,
>   mountain top, hill top,
> orchard tree, cedar tree,

beast, savage with tame,
crawler with flyer,
   prince with pauper,
boy with girl with man
   with woman, young, old,
must tell You, must tell
   You Your lovely name!
Beyond all names made!
   Lovely beyond light
of the earth or sky!
   But lavish to us,
the least of peoples!
   We live life for You!
We carry Your name!
   We tell You as well
how lovely You are!

Francis Patrick Sullivan[42]

God, Creator
and Sustainer of Life,
we the living praise You;
our hearts and our flesh
sing for joy
as we join with all of creation
in a canticle of thanksgiving
for the blessings
of the universe,
the habitat of all that lives.
Forgive our wanton
and wasteful use
of those good and precious resources
entrusted to our care.
Send forth Your Spirit,
renew the earth

as You renew its caretakers,
for we
and all of creation
cry:
Come, Creator Spirit!
Come, Soul of the Universe!
Come, Source of All that Lives!
Come, live in us!

Miriam Therese Winter[43]

God of the open garden,
we have found you
and long to hold you fast.
But you refuse our clinging need,
eluding the love
that would bind and possess you,
sending us out
beyond the bounds of our feeble knowing.

Rapt in our joy and desire,
we cannot interpret you:
you have gone from us again,
moving into morning,
moving into light.

In your great love,
wait for us
where you have sent us,
go ahead of us,
be there to meet us,
risen, released in your world.

Nicola Slee

O God, the power of the powerless,
you have chosen as your witnesses

those whose voice is not heard.
   Grant that, as women first announced the
      resurrection
    though they were not believed,
    we too may have courage
    to persist in proclaiming your word,
    in the power of Jesus Christ, Amen.

                          Janet Morley[44]

Blessed be God for the faithfulness of Mary,
   who went out from the garden
    to do her beloved's bidding,
   who joyfully proclaimed his resurrection
    to those to whom he sent her,
    and risked her self in bold believing.

In her proclamation we find courage to speak
   out.
In her acclamation we gain strength to share
    our stories.
In her vindication we know the recognition
     of our redeemed and vindicated lives.

Make us faithful like Mary,
    when faith is sent out
     into the noon of Easter morning,
Until we come at last
     to share in the full glory
      of Resurrection Day.

                          Nicola Slee[45]

EXERCISES

1   "Arise, my love, my fair one,/ and come away;/ For, lo, the winter is past,/ the rain is over and gone;/ the flowers appear on the earth;/ and the time of singing has come" (p.159). "If ever world were blessed, now it is" (p.160). Read the Song of Songs 2: 10-13 and the poem by Laurie Lee on p.159-60. Go outside and walk around your local neighbourhood. As you walk try to really attend to your environment and to notice the familiar sights and places in new ways. See what signs of spring and resurrection you can detect. Come back and jot down what you found. Pray for the people you saw, the houses you passed and for all the life represented in the places you walked.

2   Rosemary Haughton, in writing of spring and resurrection, speaks of the "violence" of spring and the "violence of absolute love which takes the kingdom by storm in a silence of total concentration" (p.164). Examine in detail this passage and the suggestive phrases used. What do they imply about Christian life? In what ways could you be more ruthless and single-minded in pursuing resurrection life? What stops you from "taking the kingdom of heaven by storm"?

3   "It was women who were first to spread the message of Easter . . . Think if women had kept silence in the churches!" (p.166). What

would have happened if the women had kept silence? Imagine Mary Magdalene leaving the garden and feeling too afraid to tell anyone what had happened. God took this risk! "In spite of the fearful precariousness of creation, God believes in the power of life which he has planted in us amid so much risk" (p.176). In what ways does God continue to entrust the future of the world into the hands of those who are few in number and low in status? In what ways does God entrust the good news of resurrection to *you*? How can you be faithful in fulfilling this trust?

4   "Things are crowding up out of the earth . . . And there are flowers uncurling and buds on everything . . . and there are primroses in the lanes and woods, and the seeds we planted are up . . ." (p.152). Go out into your garden and pick a bunch of spring flowers in full bloom, or buy some from your nearest florist. Place the flowers in a vase of water and feast your senses on them. Enjoy the variety of colour, fragrance, shape and size. Read the passage by Hildegard of Bingen on pp.176-7. Meditate on the beauty and presence of God in creation. Thank God for the new life in the world, and for the new life in you. Now think of someone nearby with whom you could share the joy of resurrection. Pray for them. Visit them, taking the flowers as a gift.

5   Read the episode from *The Secret Garden* in which Mary and Dickon take Colin into the garden (p.169). How do you imagine the garden looking, smelling, sounding, feeling? Use the passage as the basis of a guided meditation, in which you identify in imagination either with

Colin, the wounded and rejected person in need of healing, or with Mary, the one who brings someone else for whom she is concerned, to the place of healing.

6   "What you sow does not come to life unless it dies" (p.174). Examine the biblical texts on p.174-5, using commentaries to extend your own understanding of the passage. Find a quiet place and sit in front of the plant which you have tended from seed. Think back to the tiny seed from which your plant emerged. What kind of state is it in now? Is it thriving or struggling? How far does your plant correspond to your own growth? What has had to "die" in you for growth to take place?

7   "And then all will live in harmony with each other and the Earth/ and then everywhere will be called Eden once again" (p.182). Read Isaiah 35 (p.181), the passage from Judy Chicago's *Dinner Party* (p.182) and "The Kingdom" by R.S. Thomas (p.183). Reflect on the vision of the world as Eden restored in these passages. What is *your* vision of a perfectly healed and reconciled world, in which all people are happy and free? Write or paint or express in some other way this vision. Ask God to show you what you can do to begin to work towards the fulfilment of your vision in your day to day life.

8   "Now the ears of my ears awake and/ now the eyes of my eyes are opened" (p.161). Read e.e. cummings' poem on p.161. Devise a simple Easter celebration or liturgy in which you deliberately make full use of all the senses as a way

of expressing and experiencing the bodiliness of resurrection. Find ways of celebrating the Easter message of new life in sight, sound, smell, touch, taste and movement. You could use the cummings' poem as the basis for your act of celebration. Invite friends and neighbours in and throw a party afterwards as a way of sharing the Easter hope.

9   "In each brave and/ lonely story/ God's gentle life/ broke through" (p.168). Think through the major stages of your own life story. Where do you see God's hand at work? Where do you recognize the Easter process of death and resurrection? Write down or paint the major steps of your life's journey, plotting what seem to be the most significant stages so far; or you could try composing your own obituary as a way of identifying what is most important about your life story. Pray through what the Spirit reveals to you in this exercise. Thank God for being with you throughout your life's journey, reading Psalm 139 slowly and meditatively.

10 Read and make a study of *The Secret Garden*, noting especially the role that the garden plays in the healing and transformation of Mary, Colin and Ben Weatherstaff. Keep a notebook in which you jot down thoughts and reflections on the story, especially as it connects with your own life story.

Notes

INTRODUCTION

1 David Middleton, "It Was As If", in G. Bailey (ed.) *100 Contemporary Christian Poets*, Lion 1983, p.109
2 Br Ramon, *Life's Changing Seasons: Christian Growth and Maturity*, Marshall Pickering 1988, pp. 45, 9
3 Luci Shaw, "The Omnipresence", in *Postcard from the Shore*, Highland Books 1980, p.73
4 Nicola Slee, "Spring Trees at Pleshey"
5 See Matthew Fox, *Illuminations of Hildegard of Bingen*, Bear & Co. 1985, pp. 30ff.
6 Agnes Sanford, *Healing Gifts of the Spirit*, Arthur James Ltd 1949, pp. 21-3
7 Thomas Berry, "Our Children: Their Future", *The Little Magazine* 1, 10, Bear & Co., p.9
8 Br Ramon, *Life's Changing Seasons* pp. 15-16
9 R.H. Lightfoot, *St John's Gospel: A Commentary*, OUP 1960, p.322
10 Laurie Lee, "Twelfth Night", in *My Many Coated Man*, André Deutsch Ltd 1955, p.7
11 Rowan Williams, *Resurrection*, Darton, Longman & Todd 1982, pp.45, 46
12 Song of Songs 2: 10-12
13 J.M.C. Crum, "Now the Green Blade Riseth", in *The Oxford Book of Carols*, OUP 1964. pp. 306-7

1 DEATH IN THE GARDEN: The Burial

1 Frances Hodgson Burnett, *The Secret Garden*, Penguin 1951, p.23
2 Ibid., p.23
3 Ibid., p.18
4 Ibid., p.7
5 Thomas John Carlisle, "Mary Magdalene", in *Beginning*

with *Mary: Women of the Gospels in Portrait*, Grand Rapids, Michigan: Wm B. Eerdmans Publishing 1985, p.67

6   Luke 24:21

7   Mark 15:34

8   Maria Boulding, *The Coming of God*, SPCK 1982, p.40

9   Burnett, *The Secret Garden*, pp.32-4

10   John Keble, *The Christian Year*, quoted in Denys Thompson (ed.) *Readings*, CUP 1974, p.256

11   Margaret Magdalen, *Transformed by Love*, Darton, Longman & Todd 1989, pp.48-52

12   From a Mary Magdalene-tide Celebration at Southwark Cathedral, compiled by Ann Hoad

13   Michele Roberts, *The Wild Girl*, Methuen 1984, pp.96-9

14   Elizabeth Jennings, "Fantasy", in *Selected Poems*, Carcanet 1979, p.12

15   Christina Rossetti, "A Better Resurrection", in C.H. Sissons (ed.) *Christina Rossetti: Selected Poems*, Carcanet 1984, p.64

16   Ievan Ellis, "Theology of Death"

17   Kathleen Raine, "Spell Against Sorrow", in *Collected Poems*, pp.127-8

18   Neil Vivian Bartlett, "February", in *Children as Writers: Award Winning Entries from the 17th Daily Mirror Children's Literary Competition*, Heinemann 1976, p.80

19   Laurie Lee, "Twelfth Night, in *My Many Coated Man*, p.7

20   Maria Boulding, *The Coming of God*, p.34

21   Burnett, *The Secret Garden*, pp.45-7

22   Ernest Dawson, "The Garden of Shadow"

23   Brenda Norton, "On the Death of a Boy", in G. Bailey (ed.) *100 Contemporary Christian Poets*, pp.115-16

24   Nicola Slee, "Descent", in *Who are you Looking for? Easter Liturgies to launch the WCC Decade: Churches in Solidarity with Women, 1988-1998*, WICC/EFCW 1988, pp. 25-6

25   Jean Vanier, *The Broken Body*, Darton Longman Todd 1988, pp.55-6, 57

26   Laurie Lee, "Poem for Easter", in *The Bloom of Candles*, John Lehmann

27   "The Death Dirge", Ancient Celtic Prayer from Alexander Carmichael (ed.) *Carmina Gadelica*, Scottish Academic Press

28 Richard Holloway, *The Way of the Cross*, Collins Fount 1986, pp.109-10

29 Margaret Torrie, "The Question", in *Selected Poems*, CRUSE

30 Sally Dyck, "For Those in a Wintry Season", quoted in Janet Schaffran and Pat Kozak (eds.) *More Than Words: Prayer and Ritual for Inclusive Communities*, Creative Offset Printing 1986, p.58

31 Michael Marais, "Winter", in D. Hilton (ed.) *A Word in Season*, National Christian Education Council 1984, p.29

32 Maria Boulding, *The Coming of God*, pp.40-1

33 "Miss Read", *News from Thrush Green*, Penguin 1970, pp.108-9

34 Maggie Durran, *Single Parent: A Personal Story*, Lion 1986

35 Susan Hill, *In the Springtime of the Year*, Penguin 1977, p.140

36 Luci Shaw, "Faith" in *Postcard from the Shore*, p.46

37 Richard Holloway, *The Way of the Cross*, p.111

38 Donald Hilton, "The Season of Growth", in *A Word in Season*, p.27

39 Margaret Magdalen, *Transformed by Love*, pp.58-9

40 Jean Vanier, *The Broken Body*, pp.60, 63

41 Richard Sibbes, "The Bruised Reed and Smoking Flax", in Alexander Grosart (ed.) *Works of Richard Sibbes*, Edinburgh 1862-4

42 Samuel Rutherford, in Andrew Bonar (ed.) *Letters of Samuel Rutherford*, Oliphant 1891

43 Christina Rossetti, "Easter Even"

44 Myrna Reid Grant, "Plain Fact", in Luci Shaw (ed.) *A Widening Light: Poems of the Incarnation* Harold Shaw Publishers 1984, p.109

45 Br Ramon, "When the Winter of my Life", in *Life's Changing Seasons*, p.6

46 Lady Jane Grey, "How Long Wilt Thou be Absent?", quoted in B. Greene and V. Gollancz (eds.) *God of a Hundred Names*, Hodder & Stoughton 1962, pp.156-60

47 Janet Schaffran and Pat Kozak, "We Pray to You, O Promised One", in *More than Words*, p.57

48 Janet Schaffran and Pat Kozak, "Praise to You for Summer, Fall and Spring", ibid., pp.57-8

49 Taizé Collect "O God, it is your will . . .", in *Praise*

     in *All Our Days: Common Prayer at Taizé*, Mowbrays 1981, p.251

50 "Blessed be God for all the little deaths", quoted in *All Year Round 1987: Resource Material for Public Worship*, Standing Conference on Unity in Prayer, BBC 1987, pp.79-80

51 Janet Morley, "O God who brought us to birth", in *All Desires Known*, Movement for the Ordination of Women/Women in Theology 1988, p.28

52 from Dennis and Matthew Linn, *Healing Life's Hurts*, Paulist Press 1978, pp.218ff.

2 LIFE STIRS IN THE GARDEN: Mary Comes to the Tomb

1 Burnett, *The Secret Garden*, pp.61-2

2 Song of Songs 3:1-3

3 Rowan Williams, *Resurrection*, p.46

4 Burnett, *The Secret Garden*, p.71

5 Ibid., p.57-8

6 "The Earth", quoted in D. Hilton (ed. *A Word in Season*, p.48

7 Anthony Bloom, *School for Prayer*, Darton, Longman & Todd 1970, p.11

8 June B. Tillman, "Harvest of Darkness", in *Who Are You Looking For?*, p.29

9 Eugene H. Peterson, "Other Seeds Fell into Good Soil", in Luci Shaw (ed.) *A Widening Light*, p.62

10 Burnett, *The Secret Garden*, pp.68-9

11 Michele Roberts, *The Wild Girl*, pp.102-3

12 William Temple, *Readings in St John's Gospel*, Macmillan 1939-40, pp.358-9

13 David Gascoyne, "Winter Garden", in *Collected Poems*, OUP 1965, p.49-50

14 Burnett, *The Secret Garden*, pp.69-71

15 Robert Browning, "Paracelsus", quoted in V. Gollancz (ed.) *From Darkness to Light*, Victor Gollancz 1956, p.102

16 Christina Rossetti, "Spring", in C.H. Sissons (ed.) *Christina Rossetti: Selected Poems*, pp.99-100

17 Maria Boulding, *Gateway to Hope*, Collins Fount 1985, p.149

18 Br Ramon, *Life's Changing Seasons*, p.16
19 Gary Davies, "A Handful of Seed", in *A Handful of Seed*, Butler & Tanner 1983, pp.1-3
20 Jean Vanier, *The Broken Body*, pp.25-6
21 Luci Shaw, "Seed", in *A Widening Light*, p.118
22 Burnett, *The Secret Garden*, p.71
23 Nicola Slee, "Spring Trees at Pleshey"
24 Br Ramon, *Life's Changing Seasons*, p.15
25 Saunders Lewis, "Touch Me Not", in A.R. Jones & G. Thomas (ed.) *Presenting Saunders Lewis*, University of Wales Press 1983
26 Michele Roberts, *The Wild Girl*, pp.103-4
27 Rowan Williams, *Resurrection*, pp.45-6
28 Pamela Hayes, "Women and the Passion", *The Way Supplement*, Spring 1987, pp.68-70
29 William Temple, *Readings in St John's Gospel*, p.363
30 Elisabeth Moltmann-Wendel, *The Women Around Jesus*, SCM 1982, pp.70-2
31 Margaret Magdalen, *Transformed by Love*, pp.64, 74-5, 80-1
32 David Middleton, "It Was As If", in G. Bailey (ed.) *100 Contemporary Christian Poets*, p.109
33 Philippe de Grève, "Mary, weep not . . .", based on an anonymous thirteenth-century poem
34 Barbara Esch Shisler, "Poem for Easter", in Luci Shaw (ed.) *A Widening Light*, p.110
35 Andrew Young, "Nicodemus", in L. Clark (ed.) *Complete Poems of Andrew Young*, Rupert Hart-Davis 1960, pp.141-2
36 Michele Roberts, *The Wild Girl*, p.105
37 Levi Yitzchak of Beritchev, "The Dudele", quoted in J. Carden (ed.) *Another Day: Prayers of the Human Family*, SPCK 1986, p.48
38 St Anselm, "Let me Seek Thee . . ."
39 Rabbi of Ladi, "My Lord and God", quoted in B. Greene and V. Gollancz (eds.) *God of a Hundred Names*, p.230
40 Ibn 'Ata' Allah of Alexandria, "O God Seek Me", in A.J. Arberry, *Sufism*, Allen & Unwin
41 Collect for the feast of St Mary Magdalene, *The Alternative Service Book 1980*, Clowes, SPCK, CUP 1980, p.787
42 Janet Morley, "Christ our Healer", in *All Desires Known*, p.26

43 Gregory Petrov, "No One Can . . .", quoted in J. Carden, *Another Day*, pp.6-7

44 Miriam Therese Winter, "God of Power", in *Woman Prayer, Woman Song: Resources for Ritual*, Meyer Stone 1987, pp.171-2

45 George Appleton, "O Christ my Lord", in *The Oxford Book of Prayer*, OUP 1985, p.147

46 Janet Morley, "O unfamiliar God", in *All Desires Known*, p.16

47 Nicola Slee, "Blessed be God", previously published in *Who Are you Looking for*, p.9

3 SPRINGTIME IN THE GARDEN: Christ is risen!

1 Burnett, *The Secret Garden*, p.79
2 Ibid., p.107
3 Ibid., p.108
4 Ibid., pp.133-7
5 Sr Mary Agnes, "All the World Today Rings Mad with Exultation", quoted in Elizabeth Goudge (ed.) *A Book of Faith*, Hodder & Stoughton 1976, p.326
6 Rabindranath Tagore, *Creative Unity*, Macmillan
7 Rabindranath Tagore, *Gitanjali*, Macmillan
8 William Law, in S. Hothouse (ed.) *Selected Mystical Writings of William Law*, Rockliff 1948
9 H.A. Williams, *The Joy of God*, Mitchell Beazley 1979, pp.47, 49-50
10 Burnett, *The Secret Garden*, pp.167-9
11 Henry Vaughan, "The Revival", quoted in E. Goudge, *A Book of Faith*, p.56
12 George Herbert, "Easter", in C.A. Patrides (ed.) *The English Poems of George Herbert*, Dent 1974, p.62
13 Laurie Lee, "April Rise", in *The Bloom of Candles*
14 e.e. cummings, "i thank You God" in *Selected Poems 1923-1958*, Faber & Faber 1960, p.76
15 Janet Morley, "Benedicite Omnia Opera", in *All Desires Known*, pp.46-7
16 Rosemary Haughton, *The Passionate God*, Darton, Longman & Todd 1981, pp.16-17
17 Pamela Hayes, "Women and the Passion", pp.56-7

18 Miriam Therese Winter, "You Shall be my Witnesses", in *Woman Prayer, Woman Song*, p.230

19 Elizabeth Rice, "Sisters and Brothers – Arise", in I. Gjerding and K. Kinnamon (eds.) *No Longer Strangers*, World Council of Churches 1983, p.18

20 Marta Wilhelmsson, "Messengers", in *No Longer Strangers*, p.47

21 Phoebe Willetts, "Magnificat", in J. Morley and H. Ward (eds.) *Celebrating Women*, Movement for the Ordination of Women/Women in Theology 1986, p.14

22 Edwina Gateley, "The Sharing", in *Celebrating Women*, p.25

23 Burnett, *The Secret Garden*, pp.179-82

24 J.M. Neale, "Spring has come for [us] today", in M. Baughen (ed.) *Hymns for Today's Church*, Hodder & Stoughton 1982, no 160

25 J.M.C. Crum, "Now the Green Blade Riseth"

26 A sister of St Mary's Abbey, West Malling, Kent

27 Jenny Robertson, "Corn King", in J. Robertson (ed.) *A Touch of Flame: An Anthology of Contemporary Christian Poetry*, Lion 1989, p.160

28 Maria Boulding, *Marked for Life*, SPCK 1979, p.2

29 Maria Boulding, *Gateway to Hope*, p.148-9

30 Gabriele Uhlein (ed.), *Meditations with Hildegard of Bingen*, Santa Fe, New Mexico: Bear & Co. 1983, pp.49, 31, 32

31 Adapted from Sedulius Scotus, "Christ has risen . . .", quoted in Denys Thompson (ed.) *Readings*, CUP 1974, p.262

32 Sr Mary Agnes, "Easter", in *Daffodils in Ice*, Workshop Press

33 D.H. Lawrence, "The Risen Lord", in *Phoenix II: Uncollected, Unpublished and other Prose works by D.H. Lawrence*, collected and edited by W. Roberts and H.T. Moore, Heinemann 1968, p.573-75 (extracts)

34 Richard Holloway, *The Way of the Cross*, pp.118, 120-1

35 Judy Chicago, *The Dinner Party*, New York: Anchor Press/Doubleday 1979, p.256

36 R.S. Thomas, "The Kingdom", in *H'm*, Macmillan 1972, p.34

37 *Alternative Service Book 1980*

38 Taizé Collect, "Lord our God", in *Praise in All Our Days*, p.294

39 Eleventh-century Celtic prayer "Glorious Lord", from Alexander Carmichael (ed.) *Carmina Gadelica*, Scottish Academic Press

40 Teilhard de Chardin, "Thou whose brow is of snow", quoted in J. Carden (ed.) *Another Day*, p.81

41 Henry Suso, "Ah, Lord our God", quoted in J. Carden, ibid., p.18

42 Francis Patrick Sullivan, "You are Lovely, God!", in *Lyric Psalms: Half a Psalter*, Washington DC: The Pastoral Press 1983, pp.147-8

43 Miriam Therese Winter, "God, Creator", in *Woman Prayer, Woman Song*, p.164

44 Janet Morley, "O God, the power of the powerless", in *All Desires Known*, p.17

45 Nicola Slee, "Blessed be God for the faithfulness of Mary", previously published in *Who are you Looking for?*, p.9

Acknowledgements

The author acknowledges with thanks permission to reproduce copyright material as listed below.

The Bible text is from the Revised Standard Version Bible, copyright 1946, 1952, © 1971, 1973 by the Division of Christian Education of the National Council of the Churches of Christ in the USA, and is used by permission.

Gordon Bailey for "It was as if" and "On the Death of a Boy" reprinted from *100 Contemporary Christian Poets*, Lion Publishing.

Bear and Co Inc. for the extracts from Hildegard of Bingen in *Meditations with Hildegard of Bingen*, ed. Gabriele Uhlein.

The British Council of Churches for "Blessed be God for all the little deaths" from *All Year Round 1987*.

Collins Fount for the extracts from *The Way of the Cross* by Richard Holloway.

Darton, Longman and Todd for the extracts from *The Passionate God* by Rosemary Haughton, *Resurrection* by Rowan Williams, *The Broken Body* by Jean Vanier, *Transformed by Love* by Margaret Magdalen.

Gary Davies for the extracts from *A Handful of Seed*.

André Deutsch for the extracts from "Twelfth Night" in *My Many Coated Man* by Laurie Lee.

Doubleday, a division of Bantam Doubleday Dell Publishing Group, Inc., for the excerpt from *The Dinner Party* by Judy Chicago, 1979.

William B. Eerdmans Publishing Co. for "Mary Magdalene" from *Beginning with Mary: Woman of the Gospels in Portrait* by Thomas John Carlisle, 1986.

Edwina Gateley for "The Sharing" from *Psalms of a Laywoman*, published by Anthony Clarke, Wheathampstead, Herts.

Grafton Books, a Division of Collins Publishing, for "i thank You God" from *Selected Poems 1923-58* by e. e. cummings.

Hamish Hamilton for "Spell Against Sorrow" from *Collected Poems* by Kathleen Raine.

David Higham Associates for "Fantasy" by Elizabeth Jennings in *Collected Poems*.

Ann Hoad for the extracts from a Mary Magdalene Tide Celebration at Southwark Cathedral.

Macmillan for the extracts from *Readings in St John's Gospel* by William Temple.

Marshall Pickering for the extracts from *Life's Changing Seasons* by Br Ramon.

Methuen, London, for the extracts from *The Wild Girl* by Michele Roberts.

Meyer-Stone Boks, 2014 S. Yost. Ave, Bloomington, Indiana 47403, USA for "God of Power", "God Creator" and "You shall be my witnesses" from *WomanPrayer, WomanSong* by Miriam Therese Winter; and for the extracts from *More than Words* by Pat Kozak and Janet Schaffran.

Janet Morley for "O God who brought us to birth", "Christ our healer", "O unfamiliar God", "Benedicite Omnia Opera" and "O God the power of the powerless" in *All Desires Known*, Women in Theology and Movement for the Ordination of Women 1988. Available from MOW, Napier Hall, Hide Place, Vincent Street, London SW1P 4NJ.

National Christian Education Council for "Winter" by Michael Marais, "The Season of Growth" by Donald Hilton, "The Earth" from *A Word in Season*, ed. Donald H. Hilton.

Oxford University Press for "Winter Garden" © David Gascoyne 1965, 1988, reprinted from David Gascoyne's *Collected Poems 1988* (1988).

Pastoral Press for "You are Lovely God" from *Lyric Psalms: Halfa Psalter* by Francis Patrick Sullivan.

Jenny Robertson for "Corn King" from *A Touch of Flame*, ed. Jenny Robertson and published by Lion Publishing.

SCM Press for the extracts from Elisabeth Moltmann-Wendel, *Women Around Jesus*, 1962.

Scottish Academic Press for "Death Dirge" and "Benediction" from *Carmina Gadelica*, ed. Alexander Carmichael.

Secker and Warburg for "Nicodemus" by Andrew Young in *Complete Poems of Andrew Young*, ed. L. Clark.

Harold Shaw Publishers, Wheaton, Illinois 60189, USA for "Plain Fact" by Myrna Reid Grant, "Other Seeds Fell into Good Soil" by Eugene Peterson, "Seed" by Luci Shaw, "Poem for Easter" by Barbara Esch Shisler from *A Widening Light: Poems of the Incarnation*, © 1984 by Luci Shaw.

SPCK for the extracts from *The Coming of God* by Maria Boulding, © Maria Boulding; for the extracts by Levi Yitz-chak of Beritchev and Father Gregory Petrov from *Another Day*, © John Carden 1986; and for the extracts from *One Man's Prayers*, © George Appleton 1967, 1977.

Gwydion Thomas for "The Kingdom" in *H'M* by R.S. Tho-mas, © R.S. Thomas, published by Macmillan, 1972.

June Tillman for "Harvest of Darkness" from *Who are you looking for?*

Margaret Torrie MBE for "The Question" in *Selected Poems*, published in aid of Cruse, 1979. Available from Cruse.

The Way for the extracts from "Women and the Passion" by Pamela Hayes. First published in *The Way Supplement* no 58, Spring 1987.

Alfred Willetts for "Magnificat" by Deaconess Phoebe Wil-letts (1917-1978).

World Council of Churches for the extracts from "No Longer Strangers: A Resource for Women and Worship" ed. Iben Gjerding and Catherine Kinnamon 1983 WCC Publications (World Council of Churches) Geneva, Switzerland.

Fount Paperbacks

Fount is one of the leading paperback publishers of religious books and below are some of its recent titles.

- ☐ FRIENDSHIP WITH GOD David Hope £2.95
- ☐ THE DARK FACE OF REALITY Martin Israel £2.95
- ☐ LIVING WITH CONTRADICTION Esther de Waal £2.95
- ☐ FROM EAST TO WEST Brigid Marlin £3.95
- ☐ GUIDE TO THE HERE AND HEREAFTER
                             Lionel Blue/Jonathan Magonet £4.50
- ☐ CHRISTIAN ENGLAND (1 Vol) David Edwards £10.95
- ☐ MASTERING SADHANA Carlos Valles £3.95
- ☐ THE GREAT GOD ROBBERY George Carey £2.95
- ☐ CALLED TO ACTION Fran Beckett £2.95
- ☐ TENSIONS Harry Williams £2.50
- ☐ CONVERSION Malcolm Muggeridge £2.95
- ☐ INVISIBLE NETWORK Frank Wright £2.95
- ☐ THE DANCE OF LOVE Stephen Verney £3.95
- ☐ THANK YOU, PADRE Joan Clifford £2.50
- ☐ LIGHT AND LIFE Grazyna Sikorska £2.95
- ☐ CELEBRATION Margaret Spufford £2.95
- ☐ GOODNIGHT LORD Georgette Butcher £2.95
- ☐ GROWING OLDER Una Kroll £2.95

All Fount Paperbacks are available at your bookshop or newsagent, or they can be ordered by post from Fount Paperbacks, Cash Sales Department, G.P.O. Box 29, Douglas, Isle of Man. Please send purchase price plus 22p per book, maximum postage £3. Customers outside the UK send purchase price, plus 22p per book. Cheque, postal order or money order. No currency.

NAME (Block letters) _____

ADDRESS_____

_____

_____

While every effort is made to keep prices low, it is sometimes necessary to increase them at short notice. Fount Paperbacks reserve the right to show new retail prices on covers which may differ from those previously advertised in the text or elsewhere.